8.95

TRAGIC OCCASIONS

KENNIKAT PRESS

NATIONAL UNIVERSITY PUBLICATIONS

SERIES ON LITERARY CRITICISM

General Editor

EUGENE GOODHEART

Professor of Literature, Massachusetts Institute of Technology

Books By B. L. Reid

*Art By Subtraction: A Dissenting Opinion of
Gertrude Stein* (1958)

William Butler Yeats: The Lyric of Tragedy (1961)

*The Man From New York: John Quinn and His
Friends* (1968)
(Pulitzer Prize for Biography, 1969)

*The Long Boy and Others: Eighteenth-Century
Studies* (1969)

Tragic Occasions: Essays on Several Forms (1971)

B. L. REID

TRAGIC OCCASIONS

Essays on Several Forms

National University Publications
KENNIKAT PRESS
Port Washington, N.Y. • London

Library of Congress Catalog Card Number: 72-154032
ISBN 0-8046-9016-2

Manufactured in the United States of America

Published by
Kennikat Press, Inc.
Port Washington, N.Y./London

To
Roy and Margaret Finch

Preface

What finally set me going on this series of essays, all of them written between 1960 and 1965, was long intermittent brooding on two texts: Unamuno's title (more than his book), *The Tragic Sense of Life;* and W. B. Yeats's staggering remark in a letter to Lady Dorothy Wellesley, "We begin to live when we have conceived life as tragedy." Both these literary men, it was clear, were situating tragedy, without apology, in the ordinary experience of men, not only in a literary genre. It was clear too that they were thinking of more than mere pitiful happenstance and casual disaster: their view was serious and conceptual, a view of philosophical and psychological patterns, of ethical and aesthetic shapes in experience itself.

At the same time I was naturally involved, like any other student and teacher of literature, in the old hard wrestle with the formal genre, with the tragic drama and its related criticism. That struggle is endless and invigorating. But Unamuno's and Yeats's phrases set me wondering whether thought about tragedy ought to be confined to the standard dramatic examples. Was tragedy a "finished" form, as even Aristotle seemed to suppose? What had happened to tragedy in English since Shakespeare? Had it perhaps migrated to other forms, such as the novel? Why did self-consciously "tragic" contemporary plays (*e.g., Winterset, Death of a Salesman, J.B.*) fall into sentiment and bombast? Was there something distinctive and respectable that might be called the tragic sense of life, something more than *Weltschmerz*, a cast of mind or a view of the world that was carrying the power of the old tragic impulse at large into art, perhaps into unsuspected forms, and giving them their mysterious richness of meaning and feeling? It seemed to me that I could find this essence and a good many of its occasions, often in forms far removed from tragic drama: in lyric poetry, for example, and in prose fiction (even, God help me, in a comic novel).

Originally I thought to undertake a collective and comparative study, in the frame of this generic, informal sense of tragic experience, of four bodies of work, widely different in time and form, that interested me most immediately: the odes and the letters of Keats, the lyrics of Yeats, Melville's *Moby Dick*, and Sterne's *Tristram Shandy*. For various reasons I was not able to get at Melville at all at this time. But I wrote a long essay on the Keats material, nearly three times the size of the present essay, and it was already clear that I should have trouble keeping a comparative study within bounds. When I got into the Yeats poems I found the problem so complex and seductive that I resolved to let it have its way, and I went ahead and wrote a book (*William Butler Yeats: The Lyric of Tragedy*: University of Oklahoma Press, 1961), taking as validations and points of departure Yeats's two synoptic statements: "We begin to live when we have conceived life as tragedy"; and "To me the supreme aim is an act of faith and reason to make one rejoice in the midst of tragedy." There I tried to present my theory at some length and to exemplify it in analysis of Yeats's major lyrics. Meanwhile I had written and published a paper on *Tristram Shandy* holding that the special richness and resonance of comic tone in that brilliant farrago needed to be traced back to a "sense of life" that was fundamentally tragic. I soon grew uneasy about that paper, finding it overheated in style and rather shoddily supported in argument. But I still trusted my thesis, and several years later I got around to a penitential rewriting, from a different angle of attack, in an essay called "Sterne and the Absurd Homunculus" that I tried to make more temperate in style and solider in matter.

It would have been pleasant and possibly helpful, if

conscience had allowed, to have included the second Sterne essay and the summary chapter of the Yeats study within the present collection. But those papers have been printed and reprinted and that availability seems sufficient. As the collection now stands, all of the essays except the long paper on *Moby Dick* have been printed once, in slightly different forms, in quarterly literary journals. I have included a newer Yeats paper, written as a centennial tribute, instead of the chapter from *The Lyric of Tragedy*. "The House of Yeats," speaking as it does of "nobility," is less sharply pointed at the present context; but I still feel it is at home here: at heart it is still talking of the tragic sense of life, in life and work. In treating not Yeats alone but Keats and Melville as well, I find myself willingly involved, to an extent that some will call heretical, not only with their texts but with the available data of their lives. I am inquiring, after all (as they inquired of themselves), how they felt about life and how their definitions of experience impelled and colored what they wrote.

Certainly I have never wished to help to vulgarize or dilute the study of tragic theory or tragic art. I agree with Aristotle that tragedy is the highest art and that it requires systematic and perhaps reverential treatment. What I have aimed to suggest is that thought about tragedy can afford, so long as it does not lose sight of pure and original forms and principles, to proceed in a more generous and hospitable spirit, to recognize the dignity of collateral lines that still carry the family genes; and particularly to confess that the grandeur of the high art that is tragedy rests on blood-knowledge, a sense of life as primitive and ancient and stubbornly continuous as the race itself. And in the Aristotelian spirit I include here two studies of tragedies of Shakespeare, essays that are classical in principle and intention if not in stature: the pure thing remains grand and beautiful.

These six essays do not constitute or attempt a "theory of tragedy." They are critical occasions addressed to what I see as various and eminent and representative tragic occasions. I am unwilling and unable to force upon them any other kind of unity, and I hope the separate essays may be allowed merely to respect the singularity of art.

South Hadley, Massachusetts
November 11, 1970

Contents

TRAGIC OCCASIONS

Macbeth and the Play of Absolutes

I

Macbeth is one of the flawless works that tell us what art is. It is perfectly articulated, in the double sense of that word: perfectly expressed and perfectly joined. It is the shortest of Shakespeare's tragedies and the second shortest of all his plays. One comes at last to see that compactness is a form of trope for central meanings of the play. *Macbeth* is a story of crime and punishment; what it is "about" is the loss and recovery of grace. It deals with absolutes, the fullest moral absolutes available in the kingdom of this world; and supernatural extensions, hellish and heavenly, function to measure and to judge human motives and acts. In the action these absolutes are superimposed in a kind of instantaneity, almost in a single register of times and spaces. That gives the compactness its awful power—the quantity of benign and malign passion that meets the eye in a single vision. Shape, the shaping action of the moral universe upon a small, packed area in time and space, is itself signification in this play.

Macbeth is a play about the race of man and his life in time. The modes of time in the play are peculiarly complex and important. Two great persons elect to cut themselves loose from the moral base, and the result is moral and political anarchy, a total perturbation in the private mind and heart and in the life of the state. Scotland is the scene of the play, but its true world is something else, a world in the composite, medieval sense: the earth, interpenetrated by the moral cosmos, becomes the intersection of heaven and hell, the theatre of their mortal combat. All space centers upon Scotland; all time upon the present action; all men upon Macbeth and Lady Macbeth. Consider how anonymous seem the other persons in the play: aside from the two central figures, there is hardly a part that an actor of standard ego would wish to play. The time of the present action becomes representative time, all time, and Macbeth and Lady

Macbeth come to stand for the race, its possible beauty or diabolism. This is the way the concentrating force of the play works.

At one moral extreme stand the witches and damnation, at the other stand Edward the Confessor and the highest potency of human grace. Compressed within the action of the play is a calamitous spiritual history, the spectacle of the perversion, death, and damnation of the human soul. Macbeth knows simple and terrible words for his crime and its personal consequences: he has "fil'd" (defiled) his mind, and thereby his "eternal jewel given to the common enemy of man." The action displays the dark "curse" of his reign and the subterranean laboring of grace back to the light. In its implacability, the power of grace in the play is scarcely less awful than the power of evil.

The tight purposeful design of *Macbeth* works from the first words. The brief twelve lines of the witches' first ceremonial do many things. In the murky clairvoyance of their prophetical view, they set going the disruption and supervention of time that governs the meaning movement of the whole play. In their actions and in their antiphonal couplet speech, they present to the mind and to the eye the idea of pattern, of the action as a self-containing and self-fulfilling shape. Presiding as unnatural geniuses of the action, being profane chthonic spirits with familiar knowledge of the christened mortal Macbeth, they show the fatal dislocation of the moral and reasonable natural man. Above all, of course, the witches establish the spiritual atmosphere, the kind of air that is available for breathing here, in Macbeth's Scotland: "Fair is foul, and foul is fair;/ Hover through the fog and filthy air." It is a place of dense moral miasma, of collective untruth, of deceptive appearance, where the quick report of the senses must never be trusted. In Act IV Macbeth will address the witches as "secret, black, and midnight hags"; every word names an essence, a master-element, of the play, already palpable in this first little scene.

The first words of the second scene, Duncan's "What bloody man is that?" name another of these spiritual elements. *Macbeth* moves forward through blood and darkness and lurid light. The scene is composed as an inverse metaphor of action to come; Macbeth's position here will prove brutally ironic. Now he is "Valour's minion" and "Bellona's bridegroom." It is upon the rebel Macdonwald that "The multiplying villanies of nature/ Do swarm. . . ." It is "brave Macbeth" who "unseam'd him from the nave to the chaps,/ And fix'd his head upon our battlements." Macbeth, who is now the eagle and the lion, descends to become the baited bear, and in the last scene of all his severed head grins at us in grisly mimicry. The multiple ironies of the scene are collected in the captain's speech, "So from that spring whence comfort seem'd to come/ Discomfort swells." Fair is foul. The lines look immediately ahead to Duncan's trust in Macbeth's promise as supporting thane and kinsman; beyond that to Macbeth's egotistic and immoral faith that, supported by unnatural powers, he can twist an action and a state to the confirmation of his own ambition. But at the end of the scene all is triumph for Macbeth. He has "bought golden opinions" of which he is as yet ignorant; and time, moving in advance both of prophecy and of his own knowledge, has already made him thane of Cawdor.

The structure of this scene of only sixty-seven lines shows the most comprehensive of the uses of time in *Macbeth*. Shakespeare superimposes times in a macabre and unnatural co-presence, as if the whole action were present in every part, every part totally significant because it contains the whole. "In my beginning is my end," as Eliot puts it, and "in my end is my beginning." The handling of time in *Macbeth* is philosophical as well as dramatic; it makes a moral statement that becomes the thing the drama is about, what it exists to show or say. By cutting himself loose from morality, Macbeth wrenches time off its base in Scotland, and thenceforth it moves in strange, spastic, symbolic ways. The drama presents man forever involved in an ongoing moral moment in which the fate of his soul is being decided. Normally the moral moment spins on through chronological time and comes to a more or less orderly and decisive end. But in the world of this play a great man's radical criminality jars forever into now, a composite moral moment, a total spiritual panorama, spread before us with horrifying swiftness, completeness, and representativeness.

When the witches reappear to open the third scene, the effect of pattern that always accompanies them is specified as a web; the imagery suggests the weavings of motive, of plot and counterplot:

> The weird sisters, hand in hand,
> Posters of the sea and land,
> Thus do go about, about;
> Thrice to thine, and thrice to mine,
> And thrice again, to make up nine.
> Peace! The charm's wound up. (I. iii. 32-37)

The play's great theme of sleep is announced, applying now to the nameless shipman but looking on to the deep perturbation in the lives of Macbeth and Lady Macbeth. When Macbeth makes his appearance, accompanied by Banquo, his speech echoes closely the last lines of the witches from the first scene: "So fair and foul a day I have not seen." It is as if the words have lain on the filthy air, awaiting his coming. The witches hail Macbeth in the prophetic catalogue of titles that becomes a kind of litany in the later action: "Glamis. . .Cawdor. . .King. . ." The fair and foul theme recurs in Banquo's ironic question, "Good sir, why do you start, and seem to fear/ Things that do sound so fair?" His qualification, "If you can look into the seeds of time,/ And say which grain will grow and which will not," suggests the witches' prophetic powers as a perversion of normal time.

Banquo's behavior throughout the scene contrasts sharply with that of Macbeth, who immediately gives the witches delighted and fearful credence. Banquo remains natural, skeptical, resting easily within reasonable and moral limits, his own man. He addresses the witches as one "who neither beg nor fear/ Your favours nor your hate." When they have vanished, he turns to Macbeth with a question crucial to the design of the whole play: ". . . have we eaten of the insane root/ That takes the reason prisoner?" He is absolutely clear as to the unholy provenance of the witches and their wisdom. They come from "the devil"; they are "instruments of darkness" who "tell us truths,/ Win us with honest trifles, to betray 's/ In deepest consequence." Macbeth describes the witches' words as "supernatural solicitings": his phrase is blander and more dangerous. He speaks out of a fatally receptive moral neutrality. His mind has leapt to ambition's call at the witches' gorgeous forecast and at the startling confirmation, now brought by Ross, that he is already, unknowingly, thane of Cawdor. The mind, shaken, divides and equivocates; the witches "cannot be ill, cannot be good"; ". . . nothing is but what is not." Macbeth can still tell foul from fair, but he has begun to hide from himself the fact that the distinction rests on a moral absolute. He is still sufficiently in possession to know that murder is "against the use of nature." But the image of murder is one his mind can summon with terrible readiness, and entertain. Macbeth has already bit deep on the insane root that takes the reason prisoner. He is shaken in mind and soul, in reason and morality, in that "single state of man," that wholeness of being which is a harmony of intellect and morality, that radical simple unity that lets Banquo meet the powers of darkness unmoved. Twice in this scene Banquo speaks of Macbeth as "rapt." He is doubly rapt: he is enchanted, and he is possessed, siezed and taken out of himself.

The scene ends, however, neutrally and tentatively, with Macbeth ostensibly resigning his case to "chance" and "time" rather than to his own action. He makes now almost his last reference to time in a normal sense, time as an orderly ongoing continuum: "Come what come may,/ Time and the hour runs through the roughest day." Yet we feel ghastly unconscious duplicity of purpose in his speech at taking leave: "Let us toward the king."

The implied analogy of Macdonwald to Macbeth in Scene ii is repeated with powerful effect through Cawdor in Scene iv. As Duncan laments of the executed Cawdor,

> There's no art
> To find the mind's construction in the face.
> He was a gentleman on whom I built
> An absolute trust, (I. iv. 11-14)

Macbeth, foul of mind and fair of face, enters the court. It is a piece of the brilliant irony of sequence that is built into the structure of the play. In the equivocal atmosphere of treachery and triumph, the coming regicide is royally welcomed. Things intersect and overlap this way in *Macbeth*, in a telescoping of times and motives, an inextricable homogeneity. Duncan names Malcolm as heir to the throne, and Macbeth's mind and purpose leap ahead through time. As he leaves to act as Duncan's "harbinger" to Inverness, supervening Duncan's time and space, he is already envisioning a murder beyond a murder not yet committed—Malcolm's to follow Duncan's. As time now condenses toward the crime, Macbeth summons the fitting atmosphere, the shrouding and amoral night which can divide both the crime from view and the guilt from the heart—as he pitifully and brutally hopes:

> Stars, hide your fires;
> Let not light see my black and deep desires;
> The eye wink at the hand; yet let that be
> Which the eye fears, when it is done, to see.   (I. iv. 50-53)

The figure specifies the now nearly confirmed split in Macbeth's intellectual and moral nature. And the madness of the disjunction between the wish and the probability is expressed by the ironical confinement of the mad idea in the neat pattern of the couplets.

The strange effect of overlapping and overarching time marks the extraordinary scene that follows. The longer arc now is the movement of Duncan toward Inverness; it supervenes Scene v and completes itself in Scene vi. Within that curve Lady Macbeth stands at her castle, vibrating in a lust to kill and climb. Macbeth's homeward arc moves toward her. But he arrives, as it were, piecemeal, first through the letter telling of the witches' prophecy, then through the messenger who himself carries the word of a previous messenger, then through the figurative raven that hoarsely "croaks the fatal entrance of Duncan," then at last in his own flesh—all this in fifty lines. The effect is of a swift and inexorable concentration of murderous purpose upon the person of the king. Passion and resolve accumulate with terrifying speed and thickness. The Glamis-Cawdor-King ellipsis drives the action, moved by Lady Macbeth's battering imperative, "Glamis, thou art, and Cawdor; and shalt be/ What thou art promis'd." Awaiting Macbeth's coming, she makes a penetrating and brutally just analysis of his nature: "What thou wouldst highly,/ That wouldst thou holily; wouldst not play false,/ And yet wouldst wrongly win." Again we seem to hear words sounding sepulchrally through time and space, Macbeth's own, "The eye wink at the hand; yet let that be/ Which the eye fears, when it is done, to see."

Lady Macbeth brings the distortion of human nature, thus far only suggested, to abrupt and horrible perfection in this scene. By the quality of her passion and by the images she uses, she seems to leap to an immediate sympathy with the witches themselves. In effect she becomes one of them, with scarcely a transition, a familiar of the satanic powers. With a lust that is perverse and sensual, she summons them to travesty the sex that makes her human and a woman: "Come, you spirits/ That tend on mortal thoughts, unsex me here. . . .Come to my woman's breasts/ And take my milk for gall, you murd'ring ministers. . . ." She has just scoffed at Macbeth for being "too full of the milk of human kindness/ To catch the nearest way." Through her satanic familiars she summons the twin elements of the action, blood and darkness, in their most viscous forms: "Make thick my blood. . . Come, thick night,/ And pall thee in the dunnest smoke of hell. . . ." And joining in Macbeth's schizophrenic morality, she invites the night, by covering the deed, to make an insane cancellation of its reality: "That my keen knife see not the wound it makes. . . ."

Entering the scene in the midst of this inhuman speech, Macbeth incarnates the thick night. Already he seems a ghost from hell; "chastised" with the "valour" of her tongue, he will become the knife and the murdering minister. Now Lady Macbeth takes command of time and converts it all into the profane present of her irresistible will: "Thy letters have transported me beyond/ The ignorant present, and I feel now/ The future in the instant." "O, never/ Shall sun that morrow see!" she vows of the "morrow" of Duncan's intended departure. Now she forces perverted time and deceitful appearance together in a single unholy configuration:

> To beguile the time,
> Look like the time; bear welcome in your eye,
> Your hand, your tongue; look like the innocent flower,
> But be the serpent under't. He that's coming
> Must be provided for; and you shall put
> This night's great business into my dispatch,
> Which shall to all our nights and days to come
> Give solely sovereign sway and masterdom.   (I. v. 64-71)

Surely no other character in drama is so quickly, totally, and terribly present to the mind as this incredible woman.

The most beautiful and awful of the play's ironic sequences now brings Duncan to the castle. The charnel house of ravens, hell smoke, night, and inhuman beings, to his innocence and charity is a place of sweet airs and fertile influence. The lines and images flow purely and lyrically into the corrupted atmosphere:

> *Duncan.*   This castle hath a pleasant seat; the air
> Nimbly and sweetly recommends itself
> Unto our gentle senses.

> *Banquo.*   This guest of summer,
> The temple-haunting martlet does approve,
> By his loved mansionry, that the heaven's breath
> Smells wooingly here; no jutty, frieze,
> Buttress, nor coign of vantage, but this bird
> Hath made his pendent bed and procreant cradle.
> Where they most breed and haunt, I have observ'd
> The air is delicate. (I. vi. 1-10)

The exquisite courtesy with which Lady Macbeth welcomes Duncan and his train embodies their illusion of the place; it is the perfection of the fairly foul.

Now the great scene which closes this great first act takes place in a setting furnished with hautboys and torches, in a kind of twilight, tending actually and symbolically, toward the night. For Macbeth it is the twilight moment of his spirit, the continental divide of his humanity, the moment when, still in command of the data of moral choice, he must decide to be man or beast, man or devil. For the first and last time he stands fully and firmly in normal time, "But here, upon this bank and shoal of time," and looks ahead through normal time to the earthly consequences of the crime he contemplates. The clear time-sense of the moment is accompanied by a correspondingly clear moral vision; what he sees is a vision, almost apocalyptic. He deeply feels the horror of his betrayal of Duncan as kinsman, subject, and host. More deeply, he feels the horror of an attack upon a man who embodies human and royal grace. The decisiveness of the moral moment, his insight into the sacrilege of the deed, are expressed by the heroic size and strangeness of his images and their outreach into sanctity:

> . . . his virtues
> Will plead like angels, trumpet-tongu'd, against

> The deep damnation of his taking-off;
> And pity, like a naked new-born babe
> Striding the blast, or heaven's cherubim hors'd
> Upon the sightless couriers of the air,
> Shall blow the horrid deed in every eye,
> That tears shall drown the wind.   (I. vii. 18-25)

"I have no spur..." he says, and his spur appears: Lady Macbeth answers to the word as he answers to "night" in Scene v. As he hesitates on the brink she pushes him into the abyss. There follows then the crucial redefinition of "man" which functions throughout the remaining action. Stung by the valour of her tongue, he declares, "I dare do all that may become a man;/ Who dares do more is none." He dares do more than becomes a man: asserting the devil within, he descends to be less than a man. At the end of the act he is ready to "bend up/ Each corporal agent to this terrible feat": the body is to be detached from the conscience. Husband and wife part resolved to "mock the time with fairest show"—time commandeered and foul masked in fair. Two human beings, in thrall to egoistic ambition, are about to abandon reason and morality and take devilish liberties with the moral order—duty, love, kinship, law. They have yet to learn that the moral universe will tolerate no defection from the limits and obligations of the human condition. Though they seek to become devils, it will show them they are only men, and will turn and tear them in their proper flesh.

Act II moves with dreadful expedition to the murder and its consequences in the soul and in the state. Night, blood, and lurid light thicken the atmosphere until it is fairly palpable, and events labor through its viscous medium. This ultimate density will not occur again until Act V, when the sleepwalking scene

will recreate it in a way to break the heart. Now both time and
tone are conveyed with fugal intricacy by sound, noises of many
kinds. The setting is within Macbeth's castle, a night within the
night. Duncan sleeps peacefully and helplessly, his guards
drugged. Fleance's torch lights Banquo toward his bed. The
free-minded Banquo is drowsy, "A heavy summons lies like
lead" upon him, and yet he holds sleep away, his clear moral
nature mistrusting the condition of sleep in which the mind can
move free of ethical restraint: "Merciful powers,/ Restrain in me
the cursed thoughts that nature/ Gives way to in repose!" Again
Macbeth, conducted likewise by a servant with a torch, enters
the scene as if to incarnate the cursed thoughts. He invites
Banquo to future talk of the prophecy, and Banquo acquiesces,
with crucial reservation that is inversely prophetic of Macbeth's
future condition: "...but still keep/ My bosom franchis'd and
allegiance clear. . . ."

"Good repose the while!" Macbeth bids him. He can still
speak thus gracefully and in the course of nature. But the
moment he is alone, cursed thoughts present the apparition of
the dagger, "a dagger of the mind." And the mind finds the
solemn and deadly words to describe his sense of the "present
horror" of the moment before the crime:

> Now o'er the one half-world
> Nature seems dead, and wicked dreams abuse
> The curtain'd sleep. Witchcraft celebrates
> Pale Hecate's offerings, and wither'd Murder,
> Alarum'd by his sentinel, the wolf,
> Whose howl's his watch, thus with his stealthy pace,
> With Tarquin's ravishing strides, towards his design
> Moves like a ghost. (II. i. 51-56)

The physical and moral loneliness of the soul, already
abandoned in commitment to the deed, is nearly unbearable to

witness. Henceforth Macbeth is the ghost, a soul lost in the midst of life, wandering a limbo all its own, forever alien to the times and ways of men. The pace with which the ghost moves toward his design, and will move beyond it, is abstract and somnambular, timed by Lady Macbeth's summoning bell and the howling wolf.

"He is about it," says Lady Macbeth of the "fatal bellman" Macbeth, whom she has succeeded on stage. She hears the shrieking owl who succeeds the wolf of the preceding scene, as the knocking at the gate will succeed the bell. In the exchange that follows we feel Macbeth's ruination upon him, whereas his wife is resolute and seems as yet untouched. The deed which to her is a practical affair, to him has been an earthquake of the spirit. "This is a sorry sight," he says with awful simplicity of his bloody "hangman's hands." She only retorts, "A foolish thought, to say a sorry sight." The restless innocents in a neighbouring chamber have said their prayers and returned to sleep. "I could not say 'Amen'/ When they did say 'God bless us,'" Macbeth reports, in broken wonderment. It is a critical discovery. The loss of benison is a radical event in the soul and in the state. Henceforward Scotland labors to make itself again a place where men can say 'Amen' to others' 'God bless us.' Macbeth can never again say the words. Sleep becomes a pervasive and beautiful trope in the play for natural benison, the condition of earthly grace. In killing Duncan, Macbeth has destroyed the rest and ease of the soul, and the universe sends him prompt visions of the truth:

> Methought I heard a voice cry, "Sleep no more!
> Macbeth does murder sleep."—the innocent sleep,
> Sleep that knits up the ravell'd sleave of care,
> The death of each day's life, sore labour's bath,
> Balm of hurt minds, great nature's second course,
> Chief nourisher in life's feast. (II. ii. 35-40)

To each of his expressions of horror Lady Macbeth returns a busy prosaicism. "Consider it not so deeply," she says; and "Go get some water,/ And wash this filthy witness from your hand." How blandly she can speak a phrase like "filthy witness." But the "little water" which to Lady Macbeth "clears us of this deed," to Macbeth is "all great Neptune's ocean," and still less powerful to cleanse than his guilt to stain. It is the central absolute of the play: absolute guilt must carry an absolute consequence. The dreadful imperative knocking at the gate, which properly fascinated DeQuincey, is repeated ten times in this and the following scene. Lady Macbeth identifies it pragmatically as coming from "the south entry." But it "appalls" Macbeth, as it appalls us. The noise comes in fact not only from the south entry but from the world without, the whole moral cosmos, disturbed by this crime and demanding that the closed criminal world of the Macbeths open itself to inspection by the light of reason and morality. Actually and symbolically, the night is about to confront the day.

The knocking as it continues becomes a sounding signal and chronometer. It juxtaposes and measures normal time and space with time and space as distorted in the charnel house of Macbeth's castle. Thus the porter speaks ignorant truth when he plays sardonically upon the idea of being porter of hell-gate and addressing callers in the name of Beelzebub. It is hell's gate he is keeping, and his master has made himself a devil. The porter's filthy monologue is a lurid and brilliant invention of Shakespeare's, a little satyr-play in the midst of the tragedy. It functions as a quick metaphoric summary midway, expressing and embodying dramatically the corrupt and dislocated world of the action.

The regular and insistent sounds of the bell and the knocking give way to clamor and disorder when Macduff discovers the body of Duncan. "Confusion" is his word: "Confusion now hath made his masterpiece!" So personified, disorder formally enters the action as a concept and a working dramatic presence, at once moral and political: "Most sacrilegious murder hath broke ope/ The Lord's anointed temple, and stole thence/ The life o' the building!" The clamor of the bell reverberates inside an elaborate pattern of images which aims to create a metaphor of Judgment Day, a present event so terrible that it can only be understood apocalyptically. Macduff's phrases, "death itself," "the great doom's image," define the crime as a dreadful absolute. "What's the business,/ That such a hideous trumpet calls to parley/ The sleepers of the house?" Lady Macbeth demands. That trumpet, the bell, the roused "sleepers" summoned, "As from your graves rise up, and walk like spirits"—all come together in the cluster of sights and noises that compose the Doomsday vision. Eventually the whole pattern of ideas will come to bear upon Lady Macbeth's sleepwalking scene, and will thicken its meaning in a nearly insupportable way.

Macbeth's own public reaction to the sight of the king he has killed should logically be mere rhetoric and pantomine. But in making the lie he can only speak truth. We are stunned to see in his language his helpless entrapment in the criminal absolute he has created:

> Had I but died an hour before this chance,
> I had liv'd a blessed time, for, from this instant,
> There's nothing serious in mortality.
> All is but toys; renown and grace is dead;
> The wine of life is drawn, and the mere lees
> Is left this vault to brag of. (II. iii. 96-101)

The whole thing is ruined, heartbroken truth. Though Macbeth does not yet know how fully he knows it, in murdering Duncan

he has murdered sleep, time, order, meaning, the whole
sweetness of life itself. Effectually he has murdered himself, and
henceforth there is "nothing serious" in his mortality. The
blessed time is forever gone for him, a property of the innocent
past. Time for him from this point is anarchic and empty, a
waste in which he struggles in despair to restore some content of
security and significance. Explaining why he has killed Duncan's
grooms, he says that it was his "violent love" that "outrun the
pauser, reason." Again he has lied like truth; truth keeps
irrupting through policy, transforming and irradiating it. To
outrun the pauser, reason, is to take a fatal liberty with the very
anatomy of life, to cut one's tie with the root of order. Again
the radical idea is quickly specified in Macbeth's beautiful and
terrible picture of the spectacle of the murdered king, which
proves to him once and for all that the eye cannot wink at the
hand:

> Here lay Duncan,
> His silver skin lac'd with his golden blood,
> And his gash'd stabs look'd like a breach in nature
> For ruin's wasteful entrance. (II. iii. 117-120)

That is what the whole play is about, a breach in nature—how it
may come about, what consequences it brings, with what torture
it must be healed.

After the gaudy theatrical of Lady Macbeth's collapse,
followed by the flight of Duncan's sons, the act is rounded with
one of Shakespeare's characteristic little scenes of public
commentary, showing the spread of the great event out into the
general consciousness. In its way the scene is rather flat, solemn,
and conventional; yet it is full of meaning and dramatic work. It
matters a great deal, for example, that the scene turns about "an
Old Man"—nameless, an archetype. As such he can talk in terms
of the traditional time of man, and can see the extraordinary

events as the breach in nature that they are:

> Threescore and ten I can remember well;
> Within the volume of which time I have seen
> Hours dreadful and things strange; but this sore
> Night hath trifled former knowings. (II. iv. 1-4)

Ross reports the inversion of the day which follows by cosmic sympathy with the upending of the moral world:

> Thou seest the heavens, as troubled with man's act,
> Threatens his bloody stage. By th' clock 'tis day,
> And yet dark night strangles the travelling lamp.
> Is't night's predominance or the day's shame
> That darkness does the face of earth entomb,
> When living light should kiss it? (II. iv. 5-10)

The animal world has shown the same trepidation, with Duncan's horses maddened and the "falcon, tow'ring in his pride of place," who stands for Duncan, killed by the "mousing owl" who is Macbeth. We learn of Macbeth's investment as king and of the flight of the nobles. Everything in the state is "unnatural" now, "'gainst nature." And the final simply solemn couplet of the act spreads abroad that blessing which Macbeth could not speak, and which the whole state must now labor to restore:

> God's benison go with you; and with those
> That would make good of bad, and friends of foes!

Act III advances the counter-movement to that grace, the public curse embodied in Macbeth and expressed in his counter-phrase, "Things bad begun made strong themselves by ill" (III. ii. 55). Macbeth's mind is now fatally divided. His moral sense is far from dead, but it is sporadic and weak, subservient to ambition and to fear. Firmly instated in the crown but riven by guilt and doubt, he is mad to make his possession unassailable. As his public power rises, his inner control decays.

We watch with horror the coarsening and disintegration of a mind of beautiful powers.

Self-defined as he is by his profane faith in the prophecy of the witches, Macbeth's fears point first to Banquo. The act opens on the litany of titles, grated through Banquo's lips:

> Thou hast it now: King, Cawdor, Glamis, all
> As the weird women promis'd, and, I fear,
> Thou play'dst most foully for't. . . .   (III. i. 1-3)

Thereafter the action turns about his murder, Macbeth's next great forward step in blood toward "safety": "To be thus is nothing,/ But to be safely thus." Speaking in soliloquy as he awaits his two suborned assassins, Macbeth pronounces his dreadfully complete knowledge that he is henceforward a lost soul, horribly mixed with the resolve to harvest the fruits of his crime:

> For Banquo's issue have I fil'd my mind;
> For them the gracious Duncan have I murder'd;
> Put rancours in the vessel of my peace
> Only for them; and mine eternal jewel
> Given to the common enemy of man,
> To make them kings, the seed of Banquo kings!
> Rather than so, come fate into the list,
> And champion me to th' utterance!   (III. i. 65-72)

As he plots the death of Banquo and Fleance with the two murderers, we see in the fellow-feeling of the three Macbeth's quick and absolute descent. Manipulating them by power and craft, he is clearly the worst of the three. We realize that their desperation and abandonment are now expressions of Macbeth's own ruined nature. The cynicism that comes with the wreck of his morality shows in the subtle coarsening of his language. He can speak of murder now as "business" and "work"; the murder of the young man Fleance is "to leave no rubs nor botches in the work." His new low language gives an important new expression to the play's running theme of the definition of man, his right nature and its pollution. "We are men, my liege," one of the murderers protests, and Macbeth responds in terms that suggest the potential beastliness of men:

> Ay, in the catalogue ye go for men,
> As hounds and greyhounds, mongrels, spaniels, curs,
> Shoughs, water-rugs, and demi-wolves are clept
> All by the name of dogs. . . . (III. i. 92-95)

Knowledge of the beast in man is an insight that tends to come to Shakespeare's tragic heroes, Hamlet and Lear, for example. It is important that to Macbeth it scarcely comes as knowledge. The action of the play brings it to him not as metaphor but as fact, such is the disastrousness of his fall; beastliness is a thing that happens to him, not a thing that he knows.

In the second scene Macbeth and Lady Macbeth, seen alone together for the first time as king and queen, stand in a dreadful intimacy of mutual guilt and determination. Macbeth's mind is "full of scorpions"; he speaks of "these terrible dreams/ That shake us nightly." Such is now his "restless ecstasy" that he envies the king he has killed: "Duncan is in his grave;/ After life's fitful fever he sleeps well." The phrase defines what life has become for Macbeth, a fitful fever of spastic time, deprived of shape, control, proportion. Lady Macbeth, shaken as yet less deeply, can argue the specious finality of the crime: ". . .what's done is done"; and counsel confident dissembling: ". . .sleek o'er your rugged looks." The application of Macbeth's gorgeous and powerful poetry to his criminal purposes shows us the amorality which is now his way of life:

> Then be thou jocund; ere the bat hath flown
> His cloister'd flight, ere to black Hecate's summons
> The shard-borne beetle with his drowsy hums

Hath rung night's yawning peal, there shall be done
A deed of dreadful note. (III. ii. 40-44)

One of the play's greatest passages anticipates the murder of Banquo:

Come, seeling night,
Scarf up the tender eye of pitiful day,
And with thy bloody and invisible hand
Cancel and tear to pieces that great bond
That keeps me pale! Light thickens, and the crow
Makes wing to the rooky wood;
Good things of day begin to droop and drowse,
Whiles night's black agents to their preys do rouse. (III. ii. 46-53)

The uses of time are complexly polluted now. The clear light of day is enemy and alien; the night is a time of murderous work rather than of rest and sleep. "Light thickens"; the image is tactile, a limbo-light. The darkness is dense and native, summoned as mask and shield, and Macbeth's mind, hell-bound, moves through it with perfect sympathy and ghastly familiarity. He is a citizen of the witches' world now.

Banquo is killed but Fleance escapes, and when the news is brought to Macbeth in the fourth scene he finds himself still "cabin'd, cribb'd, confin'd, bound in/ To saucy doubts and fears." The appearance of Banquo's ghost at the royal banquet makes the melodrama of the scene, but the action of Macbeth's guilty and brainsick dissolution is more truly carried by the sotto-voce colloquy between husband and wife on the theme of "manliness." "Are you a man?" Lady Macbeth demands in contempt and unease. "Ay, and a bold one," he answers; it is the protest of the murderers. She shames him by calling his "flaws and starts" matter for a "woman's story at a winter's fire,/ Authoriz'd by her grandam"; calls him "quite unmann'd in folly." Macbeth addresses her and the ghost in a speech which frantically mingles adult and child, male and female, man and beast:

> What man dare, I dare.
> Approach thou like the rugged Russian bear,
> The arm'd rhinoceros, or th' Hyrcan tiger,
> Take any shape but that, and my firm nerves
> Shall never tremble. Or be alive again,
> And dare me to the desert with thy sword;
> If trembling I inhabit then, protest me
> The baby of a girl. (III. iv. 99-106)

To be everything, one must be nothing. Nothingness is what has happened to Macbeth. With the radical crime has come a "breach in nature," an evacuation of his humanity. He has lost wholeness, integrity, identity.

With his terrible clarity, he sees that he has passed the point of no return: "I am in blood/ Stepp'd in so far that, should I wade no more,/ Returning were as tedious as go o'er." Then another of his awful symptomatic pronouncements: "Strange things I have in head, that will to hand,/ Which must be acted ere they may be scann'd." Lady Macbeth counters with another of those prosaicisms which yet enclose profound truths: "You lack the season of all natures, sleep." Side by side, the two utterances exert a significant mutual force. Macbeth lacks sleep because the whole natural rhythm of his life is dislocated. His determination to move direct from thought to action, with no intervening censorship by the eye of reason or morality, makes graphic the disjunction in his moral and intellectual nature.

In the two brief scenes that round out Act III, the action moves out from this close and mad concentration to the two large contexts that enclose and qualify it. In Scene v, the hell-world of the witches reappears, with a new formality and confident power. Hecate's resolve to "draw him on to his confusion" sums up again the range of Macbeth's perturbation: "He shall spurn fate, scorn death, and bear/ His hopes 'bove wisdom, grace and fear." It is a catalogue of his abandoned values. The last scene, that between two virtual anonymities, Lennox and "another Lord," parallels the scene of Ross, Macduff, and "an Old Man" at the end of Act II, and again carries the action out into the body politic, the world of normal time and space and of merely conventionally fallen men. In the public speech Macbeth is now "the tyrant" and his criminality matter for bitter motto: ". . .men must not walk too late." We hear further of the scattering of the nobles and of the convergence now of hope upon England. The coming confrontation of curse and benison is amply specified in the speech. Macbeth's Scotland is "our suffering country/ Under a hand accurs'd!" English Edward is "pious Edward," full of "grace," "the holy king," to whom one "prays." The lost moral and political order is again wistfully embodied in the inclusive concept of "sleep":

> That by the help of these—with Him above
> To ratify the work—we may again
> Give to our tables meat, sleep to our nights,
> Free from our feasts and banquets bloody knives,
> Do faithful homage and receive free honours;
> All which we pine for now. . . . (III. vi. 32-37)

As Act II ends with a blessing, Act III ends with a prayer: "I'll send my prayers with him."

After the simplicity and single-mindedness of Act III, the fourth act is rich and complex, as tension and action accumulate about Macbeth and the forces of curse and benison gather their powers for the decisive meeting. The opening on the most elaborate and extended of the witch scenes completes the enclosure of the scene of prayer and grace within pollution from

which it must break free. About their bubbling hell-broth the
weird sisters chant rimes of a kind of absolute filthiness:

> Scale of dragon, tooth of wolf,
> Witches' mummy, maw and gulf
> Of the ravin'd salt-sea shark,
> Root of hemlock digg'd i' th' dark,
> Liver of blaspheming Jew,
> Gall of goat, and slips of yew
> Sliver'd in the moon's eclipse,
> Nose of Turk and Tartar's lips,
> Finger of birth-strangled babe
> Ditch-deliver'd by a drab,
> Make the gruel thick and slab. (IV. i. 22-32)

Macbeth's approach is signalled also in terms of a simple absolute;
he is merely "something wicked": "By the pricking of my
thumbs,/ Something wicked this way comes." Of course the
scene is set in parallel to the opening of the play; and what
terrifies us is the advancing and perfecting of the relationship
between the man and the profane spirits. Now he hails them
in terms of cynical familiarity: "How now, you secret, black,
and midnight hags!/ What is 't you do?" A witch's "familiar,"
traditionally, is one or another kind of devil.

  Punctuated by claps of thunder, the apparitions are brought
on. With an ironic momentary faith in the power of reason to
neutralize supernatural events, Macbeth briefly believes himself
confirmed in safety. There is even a moment in which he feels
he has been restored to a natural time scheme: ". . .our
high-plac'd Macbeth/ Shall live the lease of nature, pay his
breath/ To time and mortal custom." But the fourth apparition,
the show of kings, Banquo's issue, shatters his complacency
again, casts him back into life as a fitful fever, into the frantic
and irrational time-sense he has fatally earned: "Let this
pernicious hour/ Stand aye accursed in the calendar!" And now

the news that Macduff has escaped to England draws from him
another of the deadly images of time wrenched and truncated
by the mind abandoned to criminal purpose, with no
intervention of reason and morality:

> Time, thou anticipat'st my dread exploits:
> The flighty purpose never is o'ertook
> Unless the deed go with it. From this moment
> The very firstlings of my heart shall be
> The firstlings of my hand. And even now,
> To crown my thoughts with acts, be it thought and done.
> The castle of Macduff I will surprise;
> Seize upon Fife; give to the edge o' th' sword
> His wife, his babes, and all unfortunate souls
> That trace him in his line. No boasting like a fool;
> This deed I'll do before this purpose cool. (IV. i. 144-154)

Now, brilliantly, Macbeth's mad resolve is realized in the action.
With no intervention of time or event or consideration come the
firstlings of the amoral hand, the senseless murder of Lady
Macduff and her children.

In the long scene that closes the act, at Edward's court in
England, we feel the respite of escape from Macbeth's Scotland,
a grateful change in atmosphere and tempo. Men breathe a freer
air and move through time in natural ways, walking and talking
reasonably together. Like so many of Shakespeare's great scenes,
this one presents the whole play in little. It turns particularly
about the themes of grace and damnation, of manliness and
beastliness, and gives these themes some of the play's most
beautiful expressions in speech and action.

The youthful Malcolm, in his long colloquy with Macduff,
develops the strong and lovely presence of the righteous
monarch who must displace the amoral tyrant. Though he is
working a piece of complex policy made necessary by the doubt
Macbeth has placed in all men's minds, his diction is pure and

clear, informed with rectitude, largeness of spirit, love of man
and country. That purity, of motive and expression, shines
through the early lines in which, speaking of the fallibility of
men under temptation, he yet insists on the reality of the moral
absolutes:

> Angels are bright still, though the brightest fell.
> Though all things foul would wear the brows of grace,
> Yet grace must still look so. (IV. iii. 22-24)

Detailing the politic lie of his "confineless harms" surpassing the
wickedness of "black Macbeth," he tests the probity of Macduff.
He counterpoises, as does the total action of the play, the good
and evil absolutes of kingship, of humanity itself:

> The king-becoming graces,
> As justice, verity, temp'rance, stableness,
> Bounty, perseverance, mercy, lowliness,
> Devotion, patience, courage, fortitude,
> I have no relish of them, but abound
> In the division of each several crime,
> Acting it many ways. Nay, had I power, I should
> Pour the sweet milk of concord into hell,
> Uproar the universal peace, confound
> All unity on earth. (IV. iii. 91-100)

Blunt Macduff's outraged response once more underscores the
central opposition of hellish and heavenly motives:

> Fit to govern!
> No, not to live. O nation miserable,
> With an untitled tyrant bloody-scept'red,
> When shalt thou see thy wholesome days again,
> Since that the truest issue of thy throne
> By his own interdiction stands accurs'd
> And does blaspheme his breed? Thy royal father
> Was a most sainted king; the queen that bore thee,
> Oftener on her knees than on her feet,

Died every day she liv'd. Fare thee well!
These evils thou repeat'st upon thyself
Hath banish'd me from Scotland. O my breast,
Thy hope ends here! (IV. iii. 102-114)

Malcolm knows his man now, and speaks the same theme.
Macbeth is unequivocally "Devilish Macbeth," whereas "God
above/ Deal between thee and me!" And the simplicity with
which he describes his own young chastity and innocence creates
another absolute, the polar opposite of Macbeth's weary and
ramified criminality:

I am yet
Unknown to woman, never was forsworn,
Scarcely have coveted what was mine own,
At no time broke my faith, would not betray
The devil to his fellow, and delight
No less in truth than life; my first false speaking
Was this upon myself. (IV. iii. 125-131)

The scene is interrupted by a docter, a man of earthly
medicine, who describes with awe the "miraculous work" of
Edward in curing a disease called "the evil." We know the
practical meaning is scrofula, but we must not miss the force of
the generic term. There is a definite New Testament feeling
about the whole passage, and Edward's shadowy miracle-working
presence, never directly visible, carries the connotation of the
Saviour at his holy work among men. Edward in the play is
grace itself, not quite incarnate; he presides over Malcolm as the
witches preside over Macbeth. The good king's power is spoken
of entirely in terms of sanctity; he "solicits Heaven" for it, and
it is a blessed hereditary property of right kingship:

To the succeeding royalty he leaves
The healing benediction. With this strange virtue,
He hath a heavenly gift of prophecy,
And sundry blessings hang about his throne
That speak him full of grace. (IV. iii. 155-159)

Now the action again presents the moral opposites, as does the speech. Following the benign vision of Edward, Ross enters with a new review of the temporal anarchy Macbeth has made of Scotland: "...good men's lives/ Expire before the flowers in their caps,/ Dying or ere they sicken"; the grief "of an hour's age doth hiss the speaker;/ Each minute teems a new one." Reluctantly, Ross tells Macduff of the slaughter of his family. Macduff puts down his manly grief with manly resolve. The act ends with Malcolm's confident "The night is long that never finds the day." The daylight powers are ready to reclaim their own.

Lady Macbeth's sleepwalking scene at the beginning of the last act is for me the most moving and deeply disturbing short scene in all the plays. She is observed by her "waiting gentlewoman" and by a doctor, another man of earthly medicine, and we watch her over their shoulders, cold with horror. It is beautiful that what they feel is not contempt or vengefulness but pity and fear, and the human shame of witnessing the utter nakedness of a human spirit. For we realize at once that we are watching the helpless wandering of a lost soul in the vestibule of hell. What shatters us is the total transformation of her state of mind, the complete collapse of her awful will. We last saw her confident and conscienceless; now, without transition, we find her riddled and vulnerable, wide open to her guilt. Absolute humanity has again reclaimed its own, refused to allow the redefinition of the spirit as devil.

The metaphoric night that closed Act IV becomes the literal and symbolic night of this scene. The time and its confusion act as a trope for the condition of her soul, as well as for the public condition the polluted soul has set being. The proper uses of the night are disjointed by her state and her behavior. "A great perturbation in nature," says the doctor, "to receive at once the benefit of sleep and do the effects of watching." She carries a candle and "has light by her continually"; she tries to illuminate, to penetrate and deny the night, but cannot alter a night that is of the spirit. In the same way, her eyes are open but "their sense is shut." Not that she cannot see, but that she can see one thing only; what she stares at is the blinding knowledge of irrevocable guilt. And so, in her terrible public nakedness and loneliness, she moves and speaks through the catalogue of crimes. The continuing sensuous presence of the events is appalling to her and to us, the touch, the smell, the sounds of murder. All is bound up in the knowledge that guilt is beyond human remedy, unwashable, not to be made sweet. "What's done cannot be undone"—at last she knows. As the doctor phrases it, "Heaven knows what she has known"; he places her disease "beyond my practice." "More needs she the divine than the physician," he concludes.

What breaks the heart is to see that Lady Macbeth is capable of these insights and these depths of feeling, of an intensity of remorse that has effectually destroyed her in life. For that tells us what a potentially noble nature has ruined itself before our eyes. We feel the same with Macbeth, though more massively and slowly, and with the two conjoined we are granted a vision of the race itself. Looking at Lady Macbeth, the doctor sees the race and speaks for the race, our common promise, criminality, and need, of which she and Macbeth are only the beautiful extravagance: "God, God forgive us all!"

Nothing is left now but crucial action, deeds to be done by those who would make good of bad, and friends of foes. The idea of purgation and a clean new beginning is obsessive now to the end: "Meet we the med'cine of the sickly weal,/ And with him pour we in our country's purge/ Each drop of us. . . .To dew the sovereign flower and drown the weeds." The Scottish lords, marching to the battle, describe the decay of Macbeth and his power:

> Some say he's mad, others that lesser hate him
> Do call it valiant fury; but, for certain,
> He cannot buckle his distemper'd cause
> Within the belt of rule. (V. ii. 13-16)

Angus's speech is the important one here. In his repeated "Now. . .Now. . .Now," we feel the coming to bear of the collective past and its evil content upon the critical instant which will be the sum of time for Macbeth:

> Now does he feel
> His secret murders sticking on his hands;
> Now minutely revolts upbraid his faith-breach;
> Those he commands move only in command,
> Nothing in love. Now does he feel his title
> Hang loose about him, like a giant's robe
> Upon a dwarfish thief. (V. ii. 16-22)

Macbeth's condition of mind in the final scenes shows signs of both madness and valiant fury. But these are really hysterical forms of his true state, which is a condition of emptiness, a complex and beautiful vastation of spirit. His whole being has been taken over by an immense weariness and loneliness, the manifold nothingness of a man driven beyond the bearable limits of the creature. At the end the imagery carries him, in the public view, over the line into beastliness and monstrosity. But before that happens, we hear him say things that tell us once again that we are looking at the wreck of a very great humanity. The great speeches are too many, too rich, and too familiar to examine here in detail. His vision of the vanity and futility of life forms the great theme, amplified by the despair of a lost soul that knows it has earned its own damnation. Now his whole time-sense is concentrated into a single awareness of the

emptiness, the "nothing serious," of existence without that
honor he has abandoned:

> I have liv'd long enough. My way of life
> Is fallen into the sear, the yellow leaf;
> And that which should accompany old age,
> As honour, love, obedience, troops of friends,
> I must not look to have; but, in their stead,
> Curses, not loud but deep, mouth-honour, breath
> Which the poor heart would fain deny, and dare not.
>   (V. iii. 22-28)

He stands wrecked beyond hope and fear, beyond feeling.
The cry of women that signals the death of the queen scarcely
rouses him from his self-annihilating reverie. But it moves his
mind, ruminating the roots of meaning and meaninglessness, to
the greatest speech of all, so intricately simple and agonizing
that one hardly dares say it after him:

> She should have died hereafter;
> There would have been a time for such a word.
> To-morrow, and to-morrow, and to-morrow
> Creeps in this petty pace from day to day
> To the last syllable of recorded time;
> And all our yesterdays have lighted fools
> The way to dusty death. Out, out, brief candle!
> Life's but a walking shadow, a poor player
> That struts and frets his hour upon the stage
> And then is heard no more. It is a tale
> Told by an idiot, full of sound and fury,
> Signifying nothing. (V. v. 17-28)

What he wants now is death, the end of time finally understood
as emptiness and illusion. "I gin to be aweary of the sun. . . ."
The spirit is dead already, and the rest of the action is played
out by the great body and the animal courage. The imagery
insists upon the animality. Shakespeare completes the
remorseless logic of the total reduction of a nature that has

made itself inhuman. He makes Macbeth speak of his "fell of hair," and makes him resolve to die "with harness on our back." At the end he makes his own identification with the baited bear: "They have tied me to a stake; I cannot fly,/ But, bear-like, I must fight the course." Macduff vows to treat him as one of "our rarer monsters." At the end of all he is a trophy: his severed head grins through the acclamation of Malcolm and the new king's first royal speech. We recall now the beginning of the play, when brave Macbeth, Valour's minion, Bellona's bridegroom, slew the rebel Macdonwald "And fix'd his head upon our battlements." What we have witnessed in the action of the play is a moral absolute of fearful concentration and fullness, the total inversion that comes in a great nature when it detaches itself from the moral center of man.

"The time is free," Macduff announces as he bears in the head. Indeed time, in the double sense, is free. Macbeth has enslaved his time, his era; and he has wrenched and dislocated, by his sin, the normal orderly forward movement of time. We share the relief and gratitude of the new king and his new earls that we can breathe in the old natural rhythm an air purified of Macbeth's criminal presence. We applaud the right and necessary triumph of grace over malignity expressed in Malcolm's pure and stately couplets:

> What needful else
> That calls upon us, by the grace of Grace
> We will perform in measure, time, and place.
> So, thanks to all at once and to each one,
> Whom we invite to see us crown'd at Scone.   (V. viii. 71-75)

Still, it is not easy to forgive his contemptuous reference to "this dead butcher and his fiend-like queen." For that is only literal truth, not complex enough to be wholly true. Malcolm spoke better in the fourth act, when he said, "A good and virtuous nature may recoil/ In an imperial charge"; and reminded Macduff that "Angels are bright still, though the brightest fell." One of the greatest means to the powerful concentration of this play, of absolutes is the human representativeness of Macbeth and Lady Macbeth. They recall to mind what Samuel Johnson said of the human agents of Milton's great fable: "Of human beings there are but two; but those two are the parents of mankind. . . ." Both Macbeth and his Lady show us the angel and the devil that live in the soul of man, awaiting expression. Shakespeare, obviously, was thinking of the fallen Lucifer of the same fable. Macbeth falls to dark, but he falls from light.

The Last Act and the Action of *Hamlet*

II

The opening of Act V of *Hamlet* brings a shock, even to students of the plays who have grown to admire the liberties the master takes with dramatic structures, the ordinary logic of sequence. The shock is the greater for being received in the common modern forms of the play, printed or staged, which stiffen the sequence, as it were, canonize the new act *as* new, insist on both its reality and its artifice. The undivided first texts and the fluent early performances of the play, on the other hand, would doubtless have smoothed and reduced the hiatus; but they would not have removed all the shock. For the change in the tone and pace of the action is too striking, too actual not to create a problem that is still worth worrying about. Maurice Evans found the sequence so difficult, "virtually impossible to play convincingly," that he cut the Graveyard Scene completely from his "GI" *Hamlet*—"without," he says, "noticeable damage to the flow of the play." He guesses that the scene was "an afterthought," cobbled in merely to give Will Kemp a chance to show off his comic powers.[1]

Scene i of Act V is magnificent in itself, as a part, a set piece, and Evans's complacency in having abandoned it, or in having radically altered the composite form of a great work of art, is unbecoming. Still, one must sympathize with his problem, how to convey a unity that is not clear to himself. The unity is not easily clear to anybody who thinks attentively about the play. The shock really is two shocks, one being the terrible, doubly "untimely" comedy of the Graveyard, the other the astonishing change in the mood, almost in the nature, of Hamlet himself since last we saw him. His new presence, quiet, ruminative, fatalistic, strongly but easily reined in, is unexplained, unmotivated by anything we know. And these two strange sensations are offered us as matter transitional between two dramatic units that do stand in clear relationship: the close of Act IV on the plot of Claudius and Laertes to kill Hamlet in the rigged fencing match and the bare lyric notice of the death of Ophelia; and the fencing scene itself with its general carnage, "so many princes at a shot." How is the matter of Act V, Scene i related to these matters, and to the matter of the play as a whole? What, in fact, *is* "the play" and what is that "flow" of which Maurice Evans speaks? What is it that is flowing? Is this scene frivolous and extrinsic, or is it a right member of an organism so complex as to need this scene's complexity?

For the problem is not only one of the scene's "local" relevance, its work in the immediate context; the question it raises cannot be understood except in the light of the whole play, "the action" of Aristotle—that which being "imitated" forms the work of art. After praising the unity of the *Iliad* and the *Odyssey*, Aristotle goes on to generalize: ". . .so in poetry the story, as an imitation of action, must represent one action, a complete whole, with its several incidents so closely connected that the transposal or withdrawal of any one of them will disjoin and dislocate the whole. For that which makes no perceptible difference by its presence or absence is no real part of the whole" (Bywater translation). Any part of any play must meet this test of organic function. The whole Aristotelian concept of action is notoriously difficult, semantically, aesthetically, and psychologically difficult. We confuse action with plot, the suspenseful order of events; and with the plural form, actions—business, things done, things going on. We wonder how much, if at all, "the" action or "an" action is to be identified with "theme" or "meaning." I think Aristotle meant none of these things exactly yet all of them at once. The action is the corpus, the sum, formed by the events of a story so ordered as to present a particular meaning with a specific force. It is "what the story is about;" "the shape of the subject;" "the significant design."

So understood, at least, the idea has the size it needs to bear the great weight Aristotle lays upon it.

Our psychological difficulty arises from Aristotle's insistence on the primacy of action, the subordination of character. When he says, ". . .they do not act in order to portray the characters; they include the characters for the sake of the action"; or, "We maintain that tragedy is primarily an imitation of action, and that it is mainly for the sake of action that it imitates the personal agents," we feel rudely and intimately attacked. Our modern cult of personality, our faith in the importance of self-expression, finds the whole idea insulting—but peculiarly so as applied to Hamlet. For Hamlet is at once the culture-hero and the dramatic personality with whom everyone identifies with haunting intimacy—as lover, son, or second self—such is the closeness and the variety of his humanity. "After all," as Conrad's Marlowe said of Lord Jim, one of Hamlet's modern siblings, "he was one of *us*."

But Aristotle's principle of action is one of the most brilliantly true and useful in the *Poetics*. If we apply it bravely, it prohibits sentimental overemphasis on personality, misleading projection of our own needs and urges, and frees us to see the integrity of design, the over-arching power of shape, order, and proportion. "Beauty is a matter of size and order," as he says in another of his grand simplicities.

Of course the play is "about" Hamlet, there would be no play without him. But Aristotle would insist that the play is primarily an action of which Hamlet is the chief agent; what is "imitated," the objective thing that is offered us to see, is events in a significant sequence. The center of our experience is not the personality of Hamlet, Coleridgean or otherwise, but the tragic order of things that happen to him and through him. Hamlet does not summon the tragic action, Shakespeare summons him to serve it. But this is not to say that any hero would work equally well: the particular action summons the particular hero. The point comes clear at once if we try to substitute, say, Horatio for Hamlet—or Creon for Oedipus. An analogue may be of use. We can watch Henry James move from a "personal" to an Aristotelian emphasis. In his preface to *The Portrait of a Lady*, James says that the first germ of the novel lay ". . .altogether in the sense of a single character, the character and aspect of a particular engaging young woman. . . ." When he goes on to speak of his subject as "a certain young woman affronting her destiny," of his need for "positively organising an ado about Isabel Archer," of asking himself, "Well, what will she *do*?" he makes his formula more and more Aristotelian—more objective, more abstract, as it were, more in the line of action and of aesthetic shape. He is thinking of a structure surrounding Isabel Archer of due "size and order," and his subsequent metaphors in the preface are appropriately drawn from architecture. In understanding the ado about Hamlet, in *The Tragedy of Hamlet, Prince of Denmarke* or *The Revenge of Hamlet Prince Denmarke,* there is good advice in the full title. It suggests that the action of which Hamlet is agent is an affair of public moment: it is "stately", "courtly", "civic". The full title imposes the same sort of qualification as that of *Oedipus Rex*—there the agent is "the King," "Tyrannos." The ado in *Hamlet* is about a prince on princely errands; the play is not a character sketch of a brilliant but unsatisfactory young man.

If we try to borrow from *Hamlet* a Stanislavskian text or motto, an infinitive or imperative phrase to stand for the whole, as Francis Fergusson has done in defining the action of *Macbeth* (" 'To outrun the pauser, Reason' "),[2] the case proves difficult or impossible. This play's fusion of positives, negatives, and ambiguities is too complex to accommodate in a single formula—though there are phrases, "By indirections find directions out" (II. i. 66), for example, or ". . .I must be their scourge and minister" (III. iv. 175), which carry one far. And the chronicle of sheer disaster which Horatio draws up at the end is in one sense the play:

> So shall you hear
> Of carnal, bloody, and unnatural acts,
> Of accidental judgements, casual slaughters,
> Of deaths put on by cunning and forc'd cause,
> And, in this upshot, purposes mistook
> Fall'n on the inventors' heads. . . . (V. ii. 391-396)

Mr. Fergusson's formula for the action of *Hamlet* goes as follows: ". . .to identify and destroy the hidden imposthume which is endangering the life of Denmark." It is fairly satisfactory, but it does not convey much of the flavor of the play, and I must say, at some risk of paradox, that I wish to hear something of the hero: a particular action summons a particular hero. My suggestion would run as follows: "A brilliant and idealistic young prince cleanses his country and avenges his father's murder at the expense of many lives, among them his own." Let us try to trace the design of the action pointing to and beyond the problematical scene, the opening scene of the final act.

If the action is stately, having to do with the "state" of Denmark, then clearly the first scene is not a prologue but an organic member of the action, in fact a singularly forceful Aristotelian "beginning". The guards on the parapet, soon joined by Horatio, peering into the murk, putting edgy questions, speaking nervously of wars and mysteries and spirits, are types of the citizenry of the state, enacting the common condition. The melodrama of the ghost's silent first appearance dominates the movement of the scene. But that too is symptomatic, and a type of the general dis-ease and upending of things—"post-haste and romage in the land," "the night joint-labourer with the day," stars that are "sick"—that forms the climate enclosing the whole action. In another view, the crown of the scene is Marcellus' beautiful wistful picture of an opposite kind of order, the miraculous serenity of a sacred season:

> Some say that ever 'gainst that season comes
> Wherein our Saviour's birth is celebrated,
> The bird of dawning singeth all night long;
> And then, they say, no spirit can walk abroad;
> The nights are wholesome; then no planets strike,
> No fairy takes, nor witch hath power to charm,
> So hallow'd and so gracious is the time.   (I. i. 158-164)

"So have I heard and do in part believe it," answers the reasonable Horatio, and goes on to point to the arriving dawn which cleans the air and lightens the gloomy scene: "But, look, the morn, in russet mantle clad,/ Walks o'er the dew of yon high eastern hill." The watch breaks up on the resolution to tell Hamlet of the ghost. Thus the first mention of the hero comes on the energetic rising tone of the Saviour, the wholesome time, the morn, the dew on high eastern hills. The language, the words of the action, has told us what Hamlet's function is to be: he must restore the land's lost order, must "redeem the time."

Yet it is significant that we hear next not from Hamlet but from Claudius, in the first of the play's three grand court scenes. As the usurper speaks we feel at once the size of Hamlet's adversary and of his problem. The speech is a brilliant piece of public rhetoric, full of jaunty-stately turns and glides. What is most interesting in all Claudius's first speeches is the thickness of equivocation in them, the texture of paradox, ambiguity, multiplication of terms. The purpose and the effect of all this, simply, is not to reveal but to shroud truth, to hide it under the noise of verbal forms:

> Yet so far hath discretion fought with nature
> That we with wisest sorrow think on him
> Together with remembrance of ourselves.
> Therefore our sometime sister, now our queen,
> Th' imperial jointress of this warlike state,
> Have we, as 'twere with a defeated joy,—
> With one auspicious and one dropping eye,
> With mirth in funeral and with dirge in marriage,
> In equal scale weighing delight and dole,—
> Taken to wife. . . .   (I. ii. 5-14)

> What wouldst thou beg, Laertes,
> That shall not be my offer, not thy asking?
> The head is not more native to the heart,
> The hand more instrumental to the mouth,
> Than is the throne of Denmark to thy father.   (45-49)

> And now, my cousin Hamlet, and my son,—(64)

Hamlet's brutal wit catches the trick at once, and sardonically apes it: "A little more than kin, and less than kind" (65). His own first speeches, flat, precise, unequivocal, show his revulsion against the florid sophistication of Claudius. And his first speech of any length, in response to his mother's unfeeling question as to why his father's death "seems. . .so particular," is a bitter insistence on candor and right feeling, on open truth: "Seems, madam! Nay, it is; I know not seems" (76), the speech begins. And that too is one of the things the play is about, a part of its "significant design": Hamlet must restore the world's honesty of face, make it again a place where things seem what they are. If the play itself refuses us a handy motto, perhaps we may find one in a line from Wallace Stevens, "Let be be finale of seem."

The promising morn at the end of the soldiers' scene, as inductive of Hamlet, has proved a false dawn. His "nighted colour" of costume and of mind is crow-black against the peacock glitter of the court. Claudius, having royally identified himself with the state, as "the Dane" and "Denmark," leads the court off to drink "jocund health"; and the first soliloquy shows Hamlet in a mood perfectly reverse, in a condition of confused and suicidal moral nausea. The image of the sick and ambiguous world is now carried by the great trope of the "unweeded garden." The real world is not merely worse than he had grown up believing, it is foully inhuman. Compared to Claudius, his father was a demigod, "Hyperion to a satyr"; his mother has behaved less well than "a beast, that wants discourse of reason." We see a high-minded young man suffering the shock of a corrected vision of the real world. Among other things, *Hamlet* is one of the greatest of stories on the theme of initiation, a moral and intellectual ceremony in which the idealizing veil of youth is drawn aside. The shock of this corrected vision accounts in part for the savagery of the wit, a kind of murderousness, that marks Hamlet's speech at crucial points of the play, as now in the quickly ensuing passage with his friends: "Thrift, thrift, Horatio! The funeral bak'd-meats/ Did coldly furnish forth the marriage tables" (180-181).

Hamlet himself is the main subject of the interchanges in the third scene between Ophelia and Laertes and Ophelia and Polonius, and the action works ironically at this point to place the prince, in their corrupted view, in the lists of deceit and untrustworthy appearance. Hamlet's "favours" of Ophelia, according to Laertes, are "trifling," "a fashion, and a toy in blood..." (I. iii. 6). He and Polonius *assume* that "primy nature," "nature crescent," is false and seeks by trickery to work its own gross ends. In harmony with the play's pattern of ambiguous and subverted language, Polonius puns on images of commercial dealing and of clothing to slander Hamlet's motives: Ophelia has "ta'en those tenders for true pay/ Which are not sterling" (106-107); Hamlet's vows "are brokers,/ Not of that dye which their investments show,/ But mere implorators of unholy suits. . ." (127-129). Ironically, too, candor and honesty as positive subjects enter the play for the first time now in Polonius's famous charge to his son on his departure for France. Of course all these speeches rebound against the speakers: they are judged by their judgments. The effect in the action is further to isolate the young prince in an alien world; for these are the "good people" of this world, and we see them comfortably at home in the unweeded garden.

In the fourth scene Hamlet and his friends keep their cold midnight vigil for the ghost, against the background of the world in the form of the king's "rouse." In Hamlet's "swinish phrase," as Claudius "drains his draughts of Rhenish down,/ The kettle-drum and trumpet thus bray out/ The triumph of his pledge" (I. iv. 10-12). The ghost appears, and tells to Hamlet alone his tale of adultery and murder, commands vengeance, and closes with the awful admonition, "Remember me." Hamlet's response, spoken only to his own heart, is an important key to the design of the whole action:

> Remember thee!
> Yea, from the table of my memory
> I'll wipe away all trivial fond records,
> All saws of books, all forms, all pressures past,
> That youth and observation copied there,
> And thy commandment all alone shall live
> Within the book and volume of my brain,
> Unmix'd with baser matter. (I. v. 97-104)

Hamlet's vow to destroy his old "tables" and to make a new book on life, newly and terribly understood in the light of the ghost's confirmation of his worst suspicions, is another dramatic trope for the idealistic young man in the state of initiation.

More of Hamlet's bitter jesting with "this fellow in the cellarage" precedes the leave-taking from his friends. It is interesting that the parting itself is conducted in terms such as we hardly hear again until the last act, simple, candid, and calm:

> So, gentlemen,
> With all my love I do commend me to you;
> And what so poor a man as Hamlet is
> May do, t' express his love and friending to you,
> God willing, shall not lack. Let us go in together. . . . (183-187)

But the two lines that follow, their motto-function emphasized by their couplet shape, are more significant still: "The time is out of joint;—O cursed spite,/ That ever I was born to set it right!" They tell us again, apothegmatically, what we already know about the action. The young man must cleanse a filthy world.

But in destroying his old book of the world, the ghost's revelation has also destroyed Hamlet's old intellectual base. And the ghost's injunction to vengeance, no more, offers him a new vision too small and too negative to take the place of the old. The emptiness in his mind and heart, which the idea of vengeance cannot fill, helps us to understand the strange tensions in his actions henceforth. Hamlet himself, characteristically, enlarges his mission to that of redeeming "the time," the whole "state of Denmark." The *size* of his mission, so understood, goes far to explain his famous "procrastination": it is more than vengeance that he must accomplish. Yet his father has charged, "Remember me," and commanded that the memory take the form of vengeance, and Hamlet has promised. He is agitated and hampered from here on by his moral sense of the disproportion between the idea of vengeance and the idea of purgation. Hamlet is "about his father's business," but he wishes to understand his duty in the largest possible sense.

In the terms of the Aristotelian diagram, we have come to the end of the beginning. Acts II, III, and IV form what might be called the long middle and form a unit of action that we ought to treat as such. They compose a movement for which "By indirections find directions out" does indeed come close to making an adequate text. These acts, "framed" by Act I and Act V, are shaped by an intricate pattern of cross-scheming, as Claudius maneuvers to secure his false position and Hamlet seeks certainties and means in his double mission of revenge and redemption. Act II opens with Polonius's sending of Reynaldo, elaborately instructed, to test Laertes's behavior in Paris, and that passage establishes the motif of this long unit of action. Emerson in his journals speaks of Hamlet as "lined with eyes"; we can extend the figure to the whole play. Spying and testing, "assays of bias," are the characteristic motions now for a long period. Hamlet has already proposed to make use of an "antic disposition" to cover and forward his ends, and he and Horatio henceforward constantly spy upon Claudius and the court: Claudius and Polonius spend much time behind one or another arras, "seeing unseen," as they hope. The pitiful Ophelia becomes a bait for Polonius ("I'll loose my daughter to him") and in part for Hamlet. Rosencrantz and Guildenstern are imported as spies upon Hamlet, and singularly inept they prove. Polonius's attempt to sound Hamlet is rewarded with insults and satirical nonsense.

The marvelous business of the players' arrival is turned into the most complex and brilliant assay of all, the Mouse-trap, "to catch the conscience of the king," observed by Horatio "even with the very comment of [his] soul." This second of the three great court scenes is a triumph of Shakespeare's dramatic intelligence, a set piece made of planes or stages of fabrication ranging away from the viewer's eye, in complex grades of stylization and verisimilitude. We, as spectators, spy upon actors playing Hamlet and the court, observing actors playing actors playing a play, which includes both a false play and a pantomime. The dumb-show is at once the most stylized and the most primitively real, brutally "true", element of the scene: it mimes an elementary horror beyond language, which the outer frame-play, our play, is in the midst of proving possible for art after all. We can call it either the farthest or the nearest stage of reality. We are farthest from the whole, of course, just beyond Horatio, who overlooks the action with a special eye to Claudius. Hamlet himself at this point is playing a nonce-part of great intricacy, stage-managing both the outer play and the inner play, and punishing Ophelia with savage lewdness even while spying upon Claudius.

The scene is a hall of mirrors, and that in a double sense. For in fact this whole long portion of the play is marked by imagery of imagery, so to speak—mirrors, pictures, true and false faces. When Hamlet says to the player in the Mouse-trap, "Begin, murderer; pox, leave thy damnable faces and begin," he fairly spits his impatience for the thing to come to the point. "Let be be finale of seem." Hamlet's obsessive need to distinguish, and to publish, the difference between appearance and reality, the drive to come at the truth, is working everywhere now. Images of the true and the false king are invoked twice (II. ii. 380-385 and III. iv. 53-67). In the closet scene Hamlet constrains his mother to look upon her true image in "a glass/ Where you may see the inmost part of you" (III. iv. 19-20), and there she sees indeed "such black and grained spots/ As will not leave their tinct" (90-91). The falsehood of women generally, typified for Hamlet first by Gertrude and then by Ophelia, is pictured for the helpless young woman in his denunciation of the painting and dissimulation of the sex: "I have heard of your paintings too, well enough. God has given you one face, and you make yourself another. You jig, you amble, and you lisp and nick-name God's creatures, and make your wantonness your ignorance" (III. i. 148-152). But the most significant of these "mirror" images occurs in Hamlet's instructions to the players, where he asks for a performance "from the life," of photographic trustworthiness:

> Suit the action to the word, the word to the action; with this special observance, that you o'erstep not the modesty of nature. For anything so overdone is from the purpose of playing, whose end, both at the first and now, was and is, to hold, as 'twere, the mirror up to nature; to show virtue her own feature, scorn her own image, and the very age and body of the time his form and pressure. (III. ii. 19-27)

The speech, of course, defines a moral-aesthetic ideal; that it also expresses a major theme of this play, a trope for the design of its action, may be less obvious.

The "purpose of playing" is the revelation of truth, and Hamlet, who is "playing" throughout these three acts, has that moral end in view. His policy is necessary, wise, and in part pleasant to him. One side of his nature takes both physical and intellectual pleasure in the dangerous ingenuity of his strategy. As he says at the end of Act III, "O, 'tis most sweet,/ When in one line two crafts directly meet." Hamlet knows that craft is necessary, as is occasional cruelty: "I must be cruel, only to be kind" (III. iv. 178). His cruelty to Ophelia, to Gertrude, later to Rosencrantz and Guildenstern, is zestful and brilliant, like everything he does. But accompanying the zest is a profound disgust: he knows he is being forced to proceed through, and thus to share in, corrupt practices which are his object of attack. His general revulsion against his destroyed image of an ideal humanity—"And yet, to me, what is this quintessence of dust?"—is given in his early speech to

Rosencrantz and Guildenstern (II. ii. 305-322). "Use every man after his desert, and who should scape whipping?" he says to Polonius before that scene is over, not excepting himself. One act later he places himself frankly among the corrupted company:

> I am myself indifferent honest, but yet I could accuse me of such things that it were better my mother had not borne me. I am very proud, revengeful, ambitious, with more offences at my beck than I have thoughts to put them in, imagination to give them shape, or time to act them in. What should such fellows as I do crawling between heaven and earth? We are arrant knaves all; believe none of us. (III. i. 123-131)

The speech comes in a passage of bitter "antic disposition," but it carries the note of truth, of self-revelation. This real loss of a real purity, Hamlet's decline, in fact and in his own knowledge, from ideal man to real man, is one of the subtlest and most touching lines of movement in the action, a part of this play's special heartbreaking beauty. If we can see it is as cumulative, a thing that goes on from the moment Hamlet picks up the lines of revenge and purgation, we are better prepared to understand tone and meaning in that difficult last act.

The meeting of two crafts in one line is sweet to one kind of psychology; it is dangerous to all hands, and the fatal consequences of all the spying and dissembling begin to arrive. Polonius hides behind one arras too many, and finds "to be too busy is some danger" (III. iv. 33). Ophelia, broken by coarse and tricky usage, dies a suicide. Brutality as well as deviousness grows toward murder in these three acts. They are very wrong who read the action of this play as fretfully passive waiting upon events that have the quality of hysteria when they finally arrive. Deviousness, "practice," reaches a kind of crude perfection at the end of Act IV, in the scheme of Claudius and

Laertes to put an end to Hamlet: they prepare not one, but three potentially fatal devices, the "sword unbated," the poisoned tip, and the poisoned chalice. The preoccupation with death and the corruption of the body, so central in the last act, is prefigured in Act IV by Hamlet's gross treatment, in word and deed, of the body of Polonius. By the "end of the middle," we feel that the rottenness of the body politic is swollen to · bursting. We may leave it in that state for a moment in order to think about the function of a healthy member, Horatio, in the general design of the action.

Until Hamlet's death, Horatio inhabits the play with a grave and laconic placidness that one calls stoical after deciding it is not stupid. He seems to be a man of perfect emotional balance, his "blood and judgment/ . . .so well commingled" that he is "not passion's slave" (III. ii. 74-77). He is a complete integrity, absolutely sane and true. That his nature is extraordinary is the point of his function; his abnormal soundness defines the unsound norm of this world, as he stands firm amid its melodrama and moral inversion. If the play is in part a drama of initiation, it is so not only for Hamlet but for his whole visible generation—for Horatio, Ophelia, Laertes, Fortinbras, even Rosencrantz and Guildenstern. Compare the fluent heart-wholeness of the relationship of Hamlet and Horatio with the mechanistic union of Rosencrantz and Guildenstern. Shakespeare punishes their low single-mindedness by handling them as a vaudeville turn or a pair of mimes:

Claudius. Thanks Rosencrantz, and gentle Guildenstern,
Gertrude. Thanks Guildenstern, and gentle Rosencrantz. (II. ii. 33-34)

They have passed their initiation into one world, and know how to "crook the pregnant hinges of the knee/ Where thrift may

follow fawning" (III. ii 66-67). And now they must come to
cruel acquaintance with the power of outraged right, in a world
over which Hamlet begins to exercise a measure of control. The
conflict of generations within the play is one of the ways in
which it expresses the theme of initiation. The conflict is a
norm of human experience, a thing that happens to everybody;[3]
but Shakespeare here makes it into a structural member, and
thereby incorporates it into the vision of life he is imitating.
Hamlet and Claudius captain the opposed generations and the
moral destiny of the young seems to be determined by the
direction of their allegiance. Thus Horatio is important (as is
Fortinbras fleetingly at the end) in forming with Hamlet a moral
unit, an oasis of probity in the moral desert of Claudius's
Denmark. One feels that they carry about with them a little
country inside Claudius's country; they move in the loneliness of
honor. By refusing to offer a single uncorrupted person of the
older generation, the play makes the dreadful suggestion that
moral decay is an automatic concomitant of growing older. And
watching him grow wise and weary in his swift ageing, we know
that Hamlet himself is not wholly innocent.

Throughout the long middle, in any case, the center of the
action has not ceased to lie in the dramatic evocation of the
foul world, the unweeded garden, the decayed race. Its text is
most explicit in Hamlet's statement to Gertrude near the end of
Act III, in which the Christian suggestions are detailed and
surely not casual: ". . .Heaven hath pleas'd it so,/ To punish me
with this and this with me,/ That I must be their scourge and
minister" (III. iv. 173-175).

It may matter in the Christian way, among others, that the
last act opens in a Place of Skulls. One way to see the last unit
in the action is to see it as the Passion of Hamlet. Yet the act
opens as if the play had all the time in the world, and its long

first movement especially is slow and ruminative. We are returned to our original problem of the seeming disjunction and that mysterious calm that dominates the opening and indeed all but two passages in the act. If Act V does present the Passion of Hamlet, as I think it does, it does so in complex (not paradoxical) forms. But before entering the calm of this act, we need to notice that Shakespeare has already given it a subtle preparation in his treatment of the death of Ophelia. For we enter the fifth act with the excitement of the melodrama of the fourth—Hamlet's defiant response to Claudius over the death of Polonius, Ophelia's mad scenes, the enraged return of Laertes, the news of Hamlet's offstage sea fight, the new scheme for his murder—slowed and softened by Gertrude's elegiac description of Ophelia's dying and Laertes's reticent manner of accepting that news. From this point of view the approach to Ophelia's grave and the "maimed rites" of her burial in Act V form a natural and logical elision in the action.

But Shakespeare complicates that elision, and makes at once so much and so little of the grave and the burial, and this creates the problem in the unity. The body of the sweet girl is treated to more than three hundred lines—in prose—of coarse jest, travesty, forgetfulness, and ugly quarreling. The effect is both to lower and to generalize, though never to vulgarize, the total action of which this is a part. The process begins at once with the anonymity and ignorance of the gravediggers, who are nobodies from nowhere, mere men, of no provenance—the people; they give us, more loosely and less intensively than the soldiers at the beginning, the state, the mass of the body politic, the now ironic extension of the microcosm, in which for four acts we have been held tense and airless, out into the flaccid and insensitive macrocosm. In this scene we have for the first time the sense of a really "public" action, where there is space and time and people talk prose. In the second scene the play reverts to its normal constriction, its dreadful "stately" atmosphere, and the heroic and tragic quality of the action is not relieved but intensified by the interval that has come between. But the central action is going forward, in its beautifully complex way, from the first word of the act.[4]

The gravediggers help to create a theatre for the special shapes the "passion" of Hamlet is about to take. They "hold up Adam's profession" (V. i. 35); they are mere men, men of clay, and they pull the scene to the literal earth on which Hamlet walks for this time. The movement of the whole first scene, until it explodes in the quarrel at the grave, is ambulatory, processional. One thinks of Renaissance paintings, figures and actions superimposed on landscapes, as in Auden's poem. The scene is a sort of triptych, three interlinked panels. The gravediggers talk alone in the landscape, one leaves, and Hamlet and Horatio enter through the landscape to join the one who remains; the three talk, and the funeral procession enters through the landscape; Hamlet and Horatio retire to observe the ceremony, the identity of the corpse is revealed, and the quarrel ensues. We have moved from the general to the special, the imminent, tragic atmosphere.

The "subject" of all this is of course death. But death is merely the current form of the action. It is also the philosophical object of the talk, and the gravediggers, who act and speak as members of the action, help Hamlet to speak in a new philosophical way. Hamlet's mission has been to redeem the time, to "set it right," to be "scourge and minister" of the whole state. What has happened to him since we saw him off for England, I think, is that he has come to see his reading of his mission as grandiose and unreal. He sees that he himself, by reasonable standards, has been "out of joint." He is still a good man in a bad world, and he will act as heroically as a man can, but he claims no more than that. Earlier in the action Hamlet has asked, in effect, "This cup pass from me"; now he rests a mere man in the hands of God: "Not my will but thine be done."

Thus death in Act V is not primarily important in itself, or as the subject of the action, or as the object of talk; it is more important as the universal human essence, the generic shape that destiny takes, the omnipresent real. "Ay, madam, it is common," Hamlet had said to his mother long ago. In Act V, with no essential retreat from its courtliness and high heroism, the play turns into the tragedy of common life: that is, it enacts the tragic drama of human limits. It is the limited nature of man as compared to the gods or to his own aspirations that speaks, in various tones, the marvelous ironic comedy in the graveyard. It is perhaps the greatest triumph of taste over great risks in our literature. The scene shows the pitiful inadequacy of the old notion of "comic relief": the scene is not relief, not an eddy, not extraneous or superimposed in any way. It is an intensified expression of the unbroken action, an imitation in a mode almost unbearably poignant. "Death is the mother of beauty"—to borrow another motto from Wallace Stevens. The play has been throughout a gorgeous exercise of intellect and emotion, the mind and the heart; now the action, moving to complete itself, insists on its tie to the earth, and takes up the subject of the elemental body and its end, man as corpus, corpse. The ineluctable modality of the fatal, we might call it in Joycean terms. "What have you done, my lord, with the dead body?" Rosencrantz asks after the killing of Polonius; and Hamlet answers, "Compounded it with dust, whereto 'tis kin" (IV. ii. 5-6). A few lines later he shows Claudius "how a king may go a progress through the guts of a beggar" (IV. iii. 32-33).

Now the gravediggers ask, "What is he that builds stronger than either the mason, the shipwright, or the carpenter?" and answer, " '. . . a grave-maker'; the houses that he makes last till doomsday" (V. i. 46-47, 65-67).

I have spoken of the scene as a generalizing one because of its extensiveness in space and time, its cross-cutting of social strata, its ambulatory, horizontal movement; for the same reasons, and for its closeness to the plane of the earth, we might equally well speak of it as leveling. The earth is both fact and trope in the action now, and Hamlet and the clowns inhabit it equally. The typicality of the modes of death is traced out in Hamlet's ruminative reflection on the skull, finally revealed as Yorick's, which the sexton tosses up like any other troublesome stone. The grave the sexton digs is every man's and no man's; it was Yorick's and is now Ophelia's—"One that was a woman, sir; but, rest her soul, she's dead" (V. i. 146-147); it could as well be Alexander's. It is in fact the destination of human vanity: "To what base uses we may return, Horatio! Why may not imagination trace the noble dust of Alexander, till he find it stopping a bung-hole?" (V. i. 224-226). Shakespeare's point now is not merely that all men die, but that no man is great in the eye of time.

What Maynard Mack says about the "new" Hamlet of Act V seems to me just right: "It is a matter of Hamlet's whole deportment. . .the deportment of a man who has been 'illuminated' in the tragic sense."[5] Mr. Mack is right again in his account of the psychology of Hamlet's change:

> The point is not that Hamlet has suddenly become religious; he has been religious all through the play. The point is that he has now learned, and accepted, the boundaries in which human action, human judgment, are enclosed.

Hamlet has rediscovered his humanity, all of it, and that is to confess the limits of the creature. Act V insists upon death because that is the grandest, the ultimate, human limitation. But the change in the hero and the insistence upon death occur because the tragic action calls for them. Tragedy is an imitation, and what it imitates is action and life, as Aristotle says. Critics have said that in the final act Hamlet lashes out, "the serpent unwinds," at last. Certainly it is true that he performs with great efficiency, a careless, almost insolent, ease, the tasks required of him in "The Revenge of Hamlett Prince Denmarke." But this is the less significant change in the hero. The greater change is in fact an intensification of the intellectualizing Hamlet we have known all along. For Hamlet's mood throughout Act V is marked by a strange and beautiful detachment from the very acts he performs and witnesses, a sort of spectatorship or connoisseurship of life as panorama. It is essentially in that spirit that he and the play look at death in the long first scene. In this tragic vision, tragedy and comedy fuse into irony. But that is still tragedy.

Some of this irony functions even in the quarrel at Ophelia's grave, which is given a consciously histrionic turn in the epical cast of Hamlet's challenge—mocking, while enacting, human bravado:

> What is he whose grief
> Bears such an emphasis, whose phrase of sorrow
> Conjures the wand'ring stars and makes them stand
> Like wonder-wounded hearers? This is I,
> Hamlet, the Dane! (V. i. 277-281)

The histrionic motive is made specific a few lines later as Hamlet pronounces his melodramatic defiance, then pauses to point at it:

> Dost thou come here to whine?
> To outface me with leaping in her grave?
> Be buried quick with her, and so will I;
> And, if thou prate of mountains, let them throw
> Millions of acres on us, till our ground,
> Singeing his pate against the burning zone,
> Make Ossa like a wart! Nay, an thou'lt mouth,
> I'll rant as well as thou. (300-307)

This is tearing a passion to tatters, to very rags. Of course the passions that work in the scene are real, too, and they are those that inhere in the action's fatal progress. And it is wonderful to see how the encompassing design of the action accommodates these extremes of modulation. We should not miss, for example, how the prince's "This is I,/ Hamlet the Dane" echoes and displaces Claudius's similar nomination of himself in the first act. The revenge and the cleansing are going forward. But the new calmer Hamlet returns to himself in his following speech:

> Hear you, sir,
> What is the reason that you use me thus?
> I lov'd you ever. But it is no matter.
> Let Hercules himself do what he may,
> The cat will mew, and dog will have his day. (311-315)

That dignity, softened by knowledge, acidified by irony, saddened by despair, lasts out the play.

That dignity, and what I have called Hamlet's connoisseurship of the spectacle of life, the irony deepening in seriousness as the action moves toward fatality, commands the tone and the tempo now to the end. The sorting of the language to the action and its meaning, its expression of those essences, is almost incredibly fine. In a few lines of compact plain narrative, Hamlet tells Horatio of discovering Claudius's commission to England for his death, his substitution of his own counterfeit message and of Rosencrantz and Guildenstern as victims, and the sea-fight that freed him to return to Denmark. Hamlet's keen intellectual pleasure in precise and vivid speech, in words as instruments to true or false ends, shows again here in his mocking description of Claudius's "state" message and his own. The confident heart-wholeness of the new Hamlet shows in the brusque terms with which he dismisses Rosencrantz and Guildenstern to death:

> Why, man, they did make love to this employment;
> They are not near my conscience. Their defeat
> Doth by their own insinuation grow.
> 'Tis dangerous when the baser nature comes
> Between the pass and fell incensed points
> Of mighty opposites. (V. ii. 57-62)

It is instructive to compare the end of this speech with the language of a related statement at the end of Act III: "O, 'tis most sweet,/ When in one line two crafts directly meet." The juvenility, the petulance, the cant are all gone, and what remains is the blunt pragmatic confrontation. Hamlet had to touch earth to grow to adequate stature, to be able to see and to speak as above, and as in the terrible clarity of his new summary of the direct standoff of the mighty opposites:

> Does it not, think'st thee, stand me now upon—
> He that hath kill'd my king and whor'd my mother,
> Popp'd in between th' election and my hopes,
> Thrown out his angle for my proper life,
> And with such cozenage—is't not perfect conscience,
> To quit him with his arm? And is't not to be damn'd,
> To let this canker of our nature come
> In further evil? (V. ii. 63-70)

Lanuage expresses Hamlet's condition again in his easy castigation of the euphuistic Osric, whose ornate equivocation is a later sign of the "drossy age" which has been the collective enemy from the beginning.

　　Everyone has remarked Hamlet's "fatalism" (Bradley's

word) in the late action, and the text is rich in support of such a reading: heaven is "ordinant"; "There's a divinity that shapes our ends"; ". . .a man's life's no more than to say 'One' "; ". . .the readiness is all." These are great, moving, and appropriate statements; but I agree with Mr. Mack that it is Hamlet's acceptance they are appropriate to, not his fatalism. Hamlet has been demanding all through the play, "Let be be finale of seem," demanding the identification, the making-one, of appearance and reality, the bringing of things into moral focus or register. But the terms of the proposition have changed, shrunk and cooled to the scale of the real world of men. Hamlet acts out now nothing so grandiloquent as destiny, only the limits of his powers. They are heroic powers, but human ones, and they perform in the eye of God. Hamlet himself has fallen into register with the human condition.

The violent and beautiful melodrama of the sword fight, the deadly "brother's wager," the triumphant saturnalia of the occulted evil of the play's action—an event which Aristotle might have called a "probable impossibility"—precedes the elegiac close, the epiphany or showing forth of the bodies and their meaning. The "fell sergeant, Death" arrests Hamlet, Claudius, Gertrude, Laertes. Horatio is left to draw his breath in pain. We breathe with him. The best and the worst in the state have died, and the state has nearly died with them. Hamlet has brought the state out of terrible sickness at the cost of his own life. Now it is weakly convalescent. But that is not how the spectators, "You that look pale and tremble at this chance,/ That are but mutes or audience to this act" (V. ii. 345-346), feel. Our response is better rendered by the paired terms, "woe" and "wonder," of Horatio's heartbroken address to Fortinbras: "What is it ye would see?/ If aught of woe or wonder, cease your search" (373-374). The action has been an inextricable union of woe and wonder from the first lines: the events of the action make the woe; the tone and spirit of the action, shaping events into meaning to compose the significant design of the action, provide the beauty and truth to create the wonder that lets us bear the woe. The play "ends in speculation," as Keats says deep enterprises always end, the long wide look into the woe and wonder of the human condition in its grand generic forms.

We have seen the best of our time. Hamlet is not other than fatally dead. Horatio's farewell, "Good-night, sweet prince,/ And flights of angels sing thee to thy rest!" points to a cloudy region outside the competence of the dramatic action, and comforts us only with the beauty of its language. But the air is clear, and we can breathe it with pride and some confidence as well as with Horatio's pain. The action has cleared its own corrupted air through the agency of Hamlet's sacrifice, his lustration. The bad old ones at least are gone, and the visible state is left in the hands of the instructed young. We are free at last to recollect the soldier's words from the play's first scene:

> Some say that ever 'gainst that season comes
> Wherein our Saviour's birth is celebrated
> The bird of dawning singeth all night long;
> And then, they say, no spirit can walk abroad;
> The nights are wholesome; then no planets strike,
> No fairy takes, nor witch hath power to charm,
> So hallow'd and so gracious is the time. (I. i. 158-164)

But of course the only miracle that has been passed is the miracle of art. The action leaves us in the real, fallen, endlessly corruptible world, the current embodiment of the great enemy vanquished for the time by heroic courage and sacrifice. Tragedy cannot put an end to pity and fear, it can only make the terrible beautiful.

NOTES

[1] "Comments on Playing the Role of Hamlet," The Laurel Shakespeare *Hamlet* (New York, 1958).

[2] *The Idea of a Theater* (Princeton, 1949).

[3] Compare the opening of Gertrude Stein's *The Making of Americans:* "Once an angry man dragged his father along the ground through his own orchard. 'Stop!' cried the groaning old man at last, 'Stop! I did not drag my father beyond this tree.' "

[4] I am reminded of Auden's *"Musée des Beaux Arts":*

They never forgot
That even the dreadful martyrdom must run its course
Anyhow in a corner, some untidy spot
Where the dogs go on with their doggy life and the torturer's horse
Scratches its innocent behind on a tree.

[5] "The World of *Hamlet*", *The Yale Review,* XLI (1952).

Keats and the Heart's Hornbook

III

We know very well, generally speaking, why we keep reading Keats, and keep trying to find words for his touching and imposing impression upon us: his life and his work form one of the rare configurations that can define the nature of art for us. As King Lear says, in the play Keats loved best of all, "Thou art the thing itself." One is driven to one's private rereadings of the odes and the letters of Keats by their beauty, their wisdom, their difficulty, their young inconclusiveness. But these works are so familiar and beloved to students of poetry, and commentary upon them has grown so huge and expert, that one needs a good excuse for essaying yet another public rereading. Keats's love for Shakespeare is one of many hints that suggest that one profitable context for a new study is the context of the tragic.[1]

By "the tragic" I do not mean here literary, dramatic tragedy, "systematic" tragedy, the codified critical-historical fact and ideal, but something looser and more vulgar and intuitive, "the tragic sense of life," the tragedy that is "common knowledge," the ordinary thinking man's daily awareness of mutability and disaster, the discrepancy between the ideal and the real, between what life promises and what it gives: what A. C. Bradley had in mind when he acknowledged the truth, though the extra-literary truth, of the formula, "Every deathbed is the fifth act of a tragedy." This extra-literary or sub-literary or pre-literary recognition of generic tragedy has of course a great deal to do with literary tragedy when that is serious and true, for it provides tragedy's grounding in experience, blood-knowledge of the cosmic rhythm of failure and fatality.

What I propose to argue is that as Keats began to reach that tentative, yet extraordinarily impressive, height of maturity that was allowed him by the awful untimeliness of his death, the conviction that dominated his thought and his art was the radical definition of life as an affair of tragedy, and the determination to make, through art, a strict and warlike peace with life as so defined. If it is true that Keats became, in this sense, a tragic poet before he died, then it is clear that no poet. ever went a longer progress in so short a time. The "little hill" upon which he posed tremulously on "tip-toe" in the first line of the first poem in his first book was a mound of standard romantic attitudes heaped from shards of Spenser, Leigh Hunt, and a little Wordsworth. From that spongy foothold he launched out into the floating faery landscape of *Endymion*, and there he soared passionate and lost; but the next promontory he touched was high and firm, the abstract heroic country of *Hyperion* and the great odes. There "Mister John Keats five feet high" (his own description) stands monumentally. The marvelous boy had also become a tragic poet.

The case should be rested on the greatest of the odes of 1819, for those are the finest, fullest, most "finished" pieces of his work, the truest indication of the kind of thing he was now prepared and determined to write. Writing to George and Georgiana Keats in April 1819, Keats described the "Ode to Psyche," just written, as the "first and only" poem with which he had taken "even moderate pains" (II. 105).[2] He goes on: "I think it reads the more richly for it and will I hope encourage me to write other thing[s] in even a more peaceable and healthy spirit" (II. 106). The greater odes of the next few months profited by such a temper, and the internal care and the mastery they show warrant our calling them as conclusive, philosophically and artistically, as anything in Keats can be.

Ultimately, their spirit is astonishingly "peaceable and healthy," the anagnorisis of the mature tragic spirit, the record of that truce with the nature of experience which I have called strict and warlike.

Surely the best evidence we have of the "prose content" of Keats's mind as he contemplated and composed the odes, and of the order of experience of which they were an emanation, is the long journal-letter he assembled for the American Keatses between the fourteenth of February and the third of May in 1819. In Professor Rollins's edition of the letters this one fills fifty pages. In its sweep of thought, its modulation of tone and spirit, and its depth and variety of insight, the letter is one of the very richest in Keats—which is to say it is one of the richest in our language. We may try to mine it for what it tells us of the "tragic" environment of the odes.

When the letter opens, on February 14, it is two months and a half since Keats's brother Tom died of tuberculosis; at least the first sharp shock is past of that experience, in which Keats served as both nurse and mourner, and which he never really successfully assimilated. He and Fanny Brawne have now an "understanding" if not an actual engagement. If Robert Gittings is right, a fling of some sort with Isabella Jones, perhaps a fully consummated affair, is a part of recent memory. His stubborn "sore throat" is beginning to sound ominously chronic. He has recently returned from a dullish, not unpleasant, quietly productive visit to the families of Dilke and Snooks, and one of the letter's first references is to the productive side of it; in a characteristically laconic way he names one of his great poems: "I took down some of the thin paper and wrote on it a little poem call'd 'St Agnes Eve'. . . ." (II. 58). Perhaps because he is embarrassed to confess himself deeply involved in a love affair so soon after the death of Tom, Keats gives Fanny only a very casual citation: "Miss Brawne and I have every now and then a chat and a tiff" (II. 59). He reports difficulty with *Hyperion*: "I have not gone on with Hyperion—for to tell the truth I have not been in great cue for writing lately—I must wait for the sp[r]ing to rouse me up a little" (II. 62). (Before the letter is finished we are to see that the spring had roused him up to the great odes.) He performs one of his antiparsonic "rhodomontades." He gives a feeling salute to the pleasures of claret, light and bright in tone, yet in language and intensity which are to lead straight into the serious imagery of two of the odes, those to Melancholy and the Nightingale:

> . . .now I like Claret whenever I can Have Claret I must drink it.—'t is the only palate affair that I am at all sensual in. . . .if you could make some wine like Claret to d[r]ink on summer evenings in an arbour! For really 't is so fine—it fills. . .one's mouth with a gushing freshness—then goes down cool and feverless—then you do not feel it quarreling with your liver—no it is rather a Peace maker and lies as quiet as it did in the grape. . . (II. 64).

In the same "sensual" train, recollection of his other "palate passion," game—"I must plead guilty to the breast of a Partridge, the back of a hare, the backbone of a grouse, the wing and side of a Pheasant and a Woodcock passim" (II. 64-65)— reminds him that "the Lady whom I met at Hastings" (probably Isabella Jones) has been plying him so heavily with presents of game that he has been able to give much of it away.

Thus far all has been pleasant gossip and chit-chat, nothing to prepare us for the deeps to come; then they begin to arrive. Here are the last words for February 19:

> A Man's life of any worth is a continual allegory—and very few eyes can see the Mystery of his life—a life like the scriptures, figurative. . . .Lord Byron cuts a figure—but he is not figurative—Shakespeare led a life of Allegory; his works are the comments on it. (II. 67)

The passage makes several important suggestions about Keats's thinking and about the right way to read his verse. We have been repeatedly warned, new-critically, to read the poems in free-standing isolation, as naked artifacts, things-in-themselves, not to corrupt them by adducing irrelevant prose-informations. Keats's odes sustain that kind of clinical reading with nearly perfect aplomb. But this passage shows, surely, that Keats himself thought of poetry as a direct apprehension of significant experience, an entrapment in language of the "allegory" in life, its moments of fullest "figurative" gesture. Keats knew no more about the life of Shakespeare than we do; he knew a great deal of more or less accurate gossip about the life of Byron. He assumes that one is a great life, in the sense of being allegorical, figurative, and the other not great because it is not so, on the evidence of what he knows of the literature, not of the life. His assumption is gratuitous, intuitive. He speaks of what he thinks "must" be true, what he wishes to be true. Thus what he announces here is a personal ideal of literature and life and of their relation: the greatest works, the scriptural kind, are comments upon a significant, because "allegorical," life. We would do well, in reading the work of a writer who believes in this way, to make any appropriate use we can of the surrounding prose-informations.

For our context of tragedy the passage has other important information. Keats nominates as the archetype of the allegorical life, and hence as the object of highest admiration, the giant of modern tragedy, Shakespeare, whom he elsewhere wistfully summoned to be his "presidor." The view he takes of the relation between literature and personality is immensely suggestive, too. For he is not saying that literature is hotly subjective, a direct offering of the self in language, an unmodulated *cri du coeur*. It was Keats, after all, who applied to Wordsworth the devastating phrase, "the egotistical sublime."

What he asks for here, clearly, is not the exploitation of personality, but the sublimation of self into symbol, the recognition of the representative in an individual's experience: the key words are "allegory," "scriptures," "figurative." This kind of nearly classical detachment is one of the habits of mind that make one question the textbook designation of Keats as "Romantic" poet. Repeatedly in the letters, Keats speaks of "disinterestedness" as an ethical ideal, the right way for a good man to behave. In art he proposes a corollary ideal of "unobtrusiveness":

> We hate poetry that has a palpable design upon us—and if we do not agree, seems to put its hand in its breeches pocket. Poetry should be great and unobtrusive, a thing which enters into one's soul, and does not startle it or amaze it with itself but with its subject. — How beautiful are the retired flowers! how would they lose their beauty were they to throng into the highway crying out, "admire me I am a violet! dote upon me I am a primrose!" Modern poets differ from the Elizabethans in this....Why should we be of the tribe of Manasseh, when we can wander with Esau? (I. 224)

The ideal is of course specifically classical. It also seems to me specifically tragic, expressing the quality of largeness, of representativeness, of "disinterestedness," that we associate with the grandest literary tragedies, and with the tragic sense of life when that is complete and articulate.

The nineteenth of March finds Keats apparently confirmed in a mood of pleasant lassitude, "a sort of temper indolent and supremely careless." "In this state of effeminacy," he says,

> the fibres of the brain are relaxed in common with the rest of the body, and to such a happy degree that pleasure has no show of enticement and pain no unbearable frown. Neither Poetry, nor Ambition, nor Love have any alertness of countenance as they pass by me: they seem rather like three figures on a greek vase—a Man and two women—whom no one but myself could distinguish in their disguisement. (II. 78-79)

The image makes a clear presentiment of the "Ode on Indolence"; less clearly, it anticipates the "Ode on a Grecian Urn," and it may even point toward the gleaner of "To Autumn." Keats's dominant mood in this whole period is in fact as much autumnal as springlike, though one feels that he hardly knows it. Keats's poetical career is so terribly short that we almost feel that we can hold it all in a single view, and what one feels about this spring and summer of 1819 is that they form a watershed, an unsuspectedly fertile plateau, of his creative life. In this splendid garnering autumn of his youth, before that chronic "sore throat" had manifested its full fatality, he was resting and thinking and reading, savoring life and love, scorning all his work to date, and writing the best of his poems—all without knowing that his temper was anything more than "languor" and "laziness," as he called it. Had he any suspicion how short was his lease? One would like to know. I cannot avoid the feeling that a half-conscious anticipation of the end of things thickens and enriches the poems and the letters of these months.

His indolent mood is interrupted by a bit of *lacrimae rerum*, a note from Haslam portending the death of his father. This sets under way a complicated and interesting train of thought. Keats is moved first to draw up the formula of the treachery and mutability of life:

> This is the world—thus we cannot expect to give way many hours to pleasure—Circumstances are like Clouds continually gathering and bursting—While we are laughing the seed of some trouble is put into...the wide arable land of events—while we are laughing it sprouts [i]t grows and suddenly bears a poison fruit which we must pluck. (II. 79)

Then his recognition that his involvement in Haslam's grief is shallow as compared to the way he feels his own troubles makes him recall a major theme, his ideal of "disinterested" humanity:

> Even so we have leisure to reason on the misforture of our friends;
> our own touch us too nearly for words. Very few men have ever
> arrived at a complete disinterestedness of Mind; very few have been
> influenced by a pure desire of the benefit of others—in the greater
> part of the Benefactors [of]. . .Humanity some meretricious motive
> has sullied their greatness—some melodramatic scenery has fascinated
> them—From the manner in which I feel Haslam's misfortune I perceive
> how far I am from any humble standard of disinterestedness. (II. 79)

From the idealism of this he reverts to what seems a candid
acceptance of the predatory balance of the order of nature:

> For in wild nature the Hawk would loose his Breakfast of Robins and
> the Robin his of Worms The Lion must starve as well as the
> Swallow—The greater part of Men make their way with the same
> instinctiveness, the same unwandering eye from their purposes, the
> same animal eagerness as the Hawk—The Hawk wants a Mate, so does
> the Man—look at them both they set about it and procure on[e] in
> the same manner—They want both a nest and they both set about one
> in the same manner. . . . (II. 79)

Keats is adopting, for the moment, uncomfortably, the posture
of scientific "objectivity," "facing facts": "This it is that makes
the Amusement of Life—to a speculative Mind" (II. 79-80). But
this is a false posture for Keats, and he cannot hold it. The
poetic epistle to Reynolds of a year earlier records his true
native horror at the spectacle of nature seen "too deep into the
sea." He is not permanently interested in the predatory norm,
but in the heroic exceptions, the men who rise to selflessness:

> But then as Wordsworth says, "we have all one human heart"—there is
> an ellectric fire in human nature tending to purify—so that among
> these human creature[s] there is continually some birth of new
> heroism—The pity is that we must wonder at it: as we should at
> finding a pearl in rubbish—I have no doubt that thousands of people
> never heard of have had hearts comp[l]etely disinterested: I can
> remember but two—Socrates and Jesus—their Histories evince it. (II.
> 80)

Keats is trying to settle for himself, in this long portion of the long letter, a workable relation between ideality and reality, and, as several passages show, he is also trying to synthesize some heavy doses of Hazlitt's pragmatism without a sublimation unacceptable to the honesty of his own mind. The whole course of his thought here is twisting and insecure and touchingly diffident; he makes his own necessary confession of amateurishness:

> Even here though I myself am pursueing the same instinctive course as the veriest human animal you can think of—I am however young writing at random—straining at particles of light in the midst of a great darkness—without knowing the bearing of any one assertion of any one opinion. Yet may I not in this be free from sin?. . .Give me this credit—Do you not think I strive—to know myself? (II. 80-81)

Ultimately he closes this argument by shifting his direction once more; he brings back his old insistence that abstract conviction must be first "proved upon our pulses," must move through the senses and the passions: "Nothing ever becomes real till it is experienced—Even a proverb is no proverb to you till your Life has illustrated it" (II. 81). The letter rises higher later, to more secure morality and aesthetics; here what moves one is the young largeness of the mind and heart, a part of that quality Lionel Trilling, following Shaw, justly called the "geniality" of Keats.

Now he begins to feel embarrassed that he has remained so serious so long. With his typical touching magnanimity, Keats tries to lighten the weight of his own speculation for his brother and his sister-in-law by apologizing for the depth of what he has said and what he knows he is about to say:

> I am ever affraid that your anxiety for me will lead you to fear for the violence of my temperament continually smothered down: for that reason I did not intend to have sent you the following

sonnet—but look over the two last pages and ask yourselves whether I have not that in me which will well bear the buffets of the world. It will be the best comment on my sonnet; it will show you that it was written with no Agony but that of ignorance; with no thirst of any thing but knowledge when pushed to the point though the first steps to it were throug[h] my human passions—they went away, and I wrote with my Mind—and perhaps I must confess a little bit of my heart. (II. 81)

But the disclaimer doesn't really "work." It is too clear from tone and pressure in the prose and in the draft of the sonnet that the impelling "Agony" rises out of "knowledge," or at least conviction, as much as out of "ignorance." Though he deprecates the bitterness of the sonnet, its impelling emotions emerge, shamefaced but stubborn, in the phrase, "a little bit of my heart."

I take it that the sonnet itself is an important text in support of my reading of Keats as tragic poet. Its death imagery is a part of the encircling mood of the odes, where the idea of death will be variously qualified and complicated. Line eleven is a study for a central image of the "Ode to a Nightingale": "to cease upon the midnight with no pain."

> Why did I laugh tonight? No voice will tell:
>   No God, no Deamon of severe response
> Deigns to reply from heaven or from Hell. —
>   Then to my human heart I turn at once —
> Heart! thou and I are here sad and alone;
>   Say, wherefore did I laugh? O mortal pain!
> O Darkness! Darkness! ever must I moan
>   To question Heaven and Hell and Heart in vain!
> Why did I laugh? I know this being's lease
>   My fancy to its utmost blisses spreads:
> Yet could I on this very midnight cease,
>   And the world's gaudy ensigns see in shreds.
> Verse, fame and Beauty are intense indeed   ·
>   But Death intenser—Death is Life's high mead.

The blank death-wishing bitterness of such a poem does not of course define anything like the ultimate tragic vision; it embodies only its primitive grounding in the *lacrimae-rerum* landscape. But it does confess the reality of the landscape. The wonderful sentence that concludes this long entry for March 19 rounds the contradictions of Keats's "speculations" in the one perfect way, and it greatly amplifies the developing tragic vision by suggesting the crucial reconciling paradox—wholeness preserved and bitterness assimilated: "I went to bed, and enjoyed an uninterrupted sleep—Sane I went to bed and sane I arose" (II. 82). Tragedy is never fretful, never mad.

The last, particularly grand, long section of the letter begins on April 15 and ends on May 3. As usual Keats resumes with the accumulated small news of the interval of silence, and as usual the texture of the letter thickens as he exhausts his gossip and begins to dig into the current workings of his own mind. The indolent fit still grips him; nothing yet tells him that he is resting his fibres for his last great creative surge. He sounds the recurrent fiscal note of the year:

> I am still at a stand in versifying—I cannot do it yet with any pleasure—I mean however to look round at my resources and means—and see what I can do without poetry. (II. 84)

A passage of a dozen or so tantalizing lines records a shorthand version of a conversation, more properly a monologue, with the fabulous elliptical talker Coleridge, covering eighteen headings beginning with "Nightingales" and ending with "Good morning," following a chance meeting and a walk at his "alderman-after dinner pace for near two miles" (II. 88). This is succeeded by three burlesque Spenserian stanzas taking off his raffish housemate Brown—all roughly efficient ironic comedy, coming easily to the left hand, costing him little. Then he recounts a recent dream which rose out of his reading in Dante, the central image in which becomes an important figure in the "Ode to Psyche":

> The dream was one of the most delightful enjoyments I ever had in my life—I floated about the whirling atmosphere as it is described with a beautiful figure to whose lips mine were joined as it seem'd for an age—and in the midst of all this cold and darkness I was warm—even flowery tree tops sprung up and we rested on them sometimes with the lightness of a cloud till the wind blew us away again—I tried a Sonnet upon it—There are fourteen lines but nothing of what I felt in it—o that I could dream it every night. (II. 91)

He inserts the sonnet itself, the beautiful one beginning, "As Hermes once took to his feathers light," and ending, "Pale were the lips I kiss'd and fair the fo[r]m/ I floated with about that melancholy storm"—all intensely pathetic, in its ghostly half-fulfillment, as a metaphor of his star-crossed affair with Fanny. After this he makes one of his characteristic reversals of tone and directs a long passage of gusty comic raillery at Georgiana. Then, again with no warning, and with no preface except "Wednesday Evening," comes one of the capital poems, a draft of "La Belle Dame Sans Merci."

We approach now the letter's crown, the famous "vale of Soul-making" passage, a breathless paragraph which fills three and a half printed pages and closes the long entry for April 21. Keats has been reading, he says, "two very different books Robertson's America and Voltaire's Siecle de Louis xiv" (II. 100). In reflecting on these books (a total of nine volumes), he has been struck, first, by the contrast between the rude and the sophisticated society; but then, pursuing the idea, he has dredged up a revelation that has horrified him—the fact of their deeper similarity: "In How lamentabl[e] a case do we see the great body of the people in both instances" (II. 100-101). What has come to him is the conviction that the difficulty of man's estate results not from the social order but from the genes of species and fate: thus it looks irredeemable. Such, at least, is his first hypothesis, and it takes its text, we should note, from *King Lear*, showing once more how Shakespeare, and especially that play, habitually accompanied Keats in his deepest speculations:

> The whole appears to resolve into this—that Man is originally 'a poor forked creature' subject to the same mischances as a beast of the forest, destined to hardships and disquietude of some kind or other. If he improves by degrees his bodily accommodations and comforts—at each stage, at each accent there are waiting for him a fresh set of annoyances—he is mortal and there is still a heaven with its Stars abov[e] his head. The most interesting question that can come before us is, How far by the persevering endeavours of a seldom appearing Socrates Mankind may be made happy. (II. 101)

But candor drives him to say that he finds unacceptably sentimental this whole idealistic concept of human perfectibility (he has spoken patronizingly of Dilke in an earlier journal-letter as a "Godwin perfectibility Man"); the details in which he amplifies his pragmatic disenchantment crudely dramatize the impossibility of earthly well-being:

> But in truth I do not at all believe in this sort of perfectibility—the nature of the world will not admit of it—the inhabitants of the world will correspond to itself—Let the fish philosophise the ice away from the Rivers in winter time and they shall be at continual play in the tepid delight of summer. Look at the Poles and at the sands of Africa, Whirlpools and volcanoes—Let men exterminate them and I will say that they may arrive at earthly Happiness—The point at which Man may arrive is as far as the paralel state in inanimate nature and no further—For instance suppose a rose to have sensation, it blooms on a beautiful morning it enjoys itself—but there comes a cold wind, a hot sun—it cannot escape it, it cannot destroy its annoyances—they are as native to the world as itself: no more can man be happy in spite, the world[l]y elements will prey upon his nature. (II. 101)

The passage that follows contains the heart of Keats as man, as thinker, and as tragic poet. It forms a complicated web of rejections and acceptances. He has already rejected the adolescent notion of the world as a place of sentimental felicity. He now rejects the conclusion that would seem to follow, that life on earth is only a drab and hopeless interregnum; he then specifically rejects the Christian corollary of that view, that we are rescued from the interregnum by a *deus ex machina* immortality. He now posits his great acceptances—of death as the limit of life, of the enmity of fate to the individual, of the duty of man to assemble his joy out of the parts of his being infallibly scattered by the Furies of destiny. The first lines of the passage summarize the whole argument:

> The common cognomen of this world among the misguided and superstitious is 'a vale of tears' from which we are to be redeemed by a certain arbit[r]ary interposition of God and taken to Heaven—What a little circumscribe[d] straightened notion! Call the world if you Please "The vale of Soul-making" Then you will find out the use of the world....(II. 101-102)

Keats then labors to clarify his use of "Soul." He equates it, we see, with "identity"; but by identity he means something larger than "personality," or consciousness of self: he means, in fact, almost the opposite—an assembled wholeness, an achieved invulnerability. The "bliss peculiar to each ones individual existence" is the joyous sense of that wholeness; and the proper "use of the world," the world that we know, is that only such a world can provide a discipline rigorous enough to accomplish such wholeness.

> ...I say 'Soul making' Soul as distinguished from an Intelligence—There may be intelligences or sparks of the divinity in millions—but they are not Souls...till they acquire identities, till each one is personally itself....How then are these sparks which are God to have identity given them—so as ever to posses a bliss peculiar to each ones individual existence? How, but by the medium of a world

like this? This point I sincerely wish to consider because I think it a grander system of salvation than the chrysteain religion—or rather it is a system of Spirit-creation. (II. 102)

He then sums up his speculation in a figure of splendid simplicity:

> I will call the world a School instituted for the purpose of teaching little children to read—I will call the human heart the horn book used in that School—and I will call the Child able to read, the Soul made from that school and its hornbook. Do you not see how necessary a World of Pains and troubles is to school an Intelligence and make it a soul? A Place where the heart must feel and suffer in a thousand diverse ways! Not merely is the Heart a Hornbook, It is the Minds Bible, it is the Minds experience, it is the teat from which the Mind or intelligence sucks its identity....This appears to me a faint sketch of a system of Salvation which does not affront our reason and humanity. (II. 102-103)

Finally, fearing he still has not made himself clear, Keats goes on to recapitulate his whole argument.

Drafts of poems fill most of the remaining pages of the long letter—two mediocre sonnets on Fame, the beautiful sonnet "To Sleep," which begins, "O soft embalmer of the still midnight," and ends with the dark velvet lines, "Turn the key deftly in the oiled wards/ And seal the hushed Casket of my Soul," the final sonnet an experiment in getting rid of the "pouncing rhymes" of the conventional form, which points toward the great ode stanza now forming in the work of these spring days. Then this magnificent letter ends with a serene image of the season itself, an image which reappears in the "Ode to a Nightingale," and which forms as well a perfect figure for that mood of calm transcendence which makes one of the last movements in the "tragic" sequence: "...this is the 3 of May and every thing is in delightful forwardness; the violets are not withered, before the peeping of the first rose...." (II. 109). We may discover in the lines "To Sleep," in Keats's setting for the "Ode to Psyche," and in the draft of the ode itself that immediately follows, the kind of poetry that was beginning to come out of the deep philosophical equipoise at which he had arrived in the thought of these months.

It is difficult not to claim too much for such an appealing document as this letter, but it is also important to claim enough. This is after all not a finished essay in ethics or aesthetics, and Keats was after all a very young man. But, though he was half-lettered, he was also an extraordinarily brilliant and high-principled young man. And so, though the thought here is often rude or incomplete, or merely derivative (especially from Hazlitt and Locke), it is also strangely mellow, beautifully intelligent, and movingly humane. We have already seen Keats's own exactly proper apology: "I am however young writing at random—straining at particles of light in the midst of a great darkness. . . .Yet may I not in this be free from sin?" I am far from claiming that Keats was putting together here anything like a conscious or coherent "theory of tragedy"; what I do suggest is that this most comprehensive of all the prose expressions of Keats's "sense of life" assembles a definition of experience as a generically-tragic order, and that this, the most conclusive view of life he lived to record, formed the subject matter and the impelling emotion of the greatest of his odes. These are the major motives in Keats's tragic sense of life as I see them emerging in the letter: a high-serious "Melancholy," recognizing the world as a place of immanent defeat and death; the invocation of Shakespeare as his "presidor"; the criterion of "disinterestedness," calling for objective selflessness and a clinical use of personal experience as "figurative"—representative and symbolic; his agnostic rejection of other-worldly solutions of tragic fact, and the determination to use the resources of the mind and heart in this world to make a viable peace with fatal reality; the general compelling tendency to reconcile the complex sadness of experience in an oxymoronic tragic joy—"the bitter Sweet of this Shakespearean fruit," as he called it in his sonnet on *King Lear*. Most of these motives are finely compressed in a sentence in a famous letter to Reynolds: "Until we are sick, we understand not;—in fine, as Byron says, 'Knowledge is Sorrow;' and I go on to say that "Sorrow is Wisdom"—and further for aught we can know for certainty! "Wisdom is folly. . . ." (I. 279).

The awful telescoping of Keats's life forced this kind of insight upon him. The marvelous thing is the balance; never, at least never until the end when his emotional control began to go to pieces with the dissolution of his body, was his passion ever sour or frantic. The serenely disciplined poise of it all, the sweetness, is intensely moving to witness. Writing to Shelley, whose behavior to Keats was beautiful throughout, and who had written to offer a haven in Italy to the young poet dying of the "disease particularly fond of people who write such good verses as you have done," Keats embodied his inner reconciliation, his complicated peace, in one of the finest of his figures: "My Imagination is a Monastry and I am its Monk" (II. 323). "Extraordina[r]y talk for the writer of Endymion," as he himself notes. But Keats in 1820 was not merely the writer of that "green tangle," as Bridges called it; he was the composer of the ode "To Autumn": he was "pick'd up and sorted to a pip."

II

It is wise to give in at once to the temptation to think of Keats's great odes of 1819 as in essence a single long poem—or at least, as Professor Garrod suggested, as an "ode-sequence." But I insist that one must not detach "To Autumn" from the sequence, as Garrod and most other commentators like to do; though it comes later by a few months, it is in every way a vital part of the total organism. It is certain that Keats did not think of his odes as one poem, and very likely that he did not think of them as an organic sequence. But in our aloofness from the creative act, we are entitled to specify the relatedness in tone and theme that was probably half-conscious for Keats; and so long as we do not destroy the integrity of the odes as separate poems we will profit legitimately from the light that comes from reading them as a composite work of art.

Indeed I should like to impose a still tighter and more arbitrary pattern—because I think the pattern exists in fact and, by marking the major stages in the definition of Keats as tragic poet, reveals a crucial truth. That pattern eliminates the "Ode to Psyche" and the "Ode on Indolence" and is composed of, in order, the "Ode on Melancholy," the "Ode to a Nightingale," the "Ode on a Grecian Urn," and "To Autumn." Yet it is very important to see that the generating mood of all the odes originates, however unpromisingly, in the "Ode on Indolence." Keats's mood of dreamy lassitude, which is described so often in the letters of 1819, and which is met in this poem in "Ripe was the drowsy hour;/ The blissful cloud of summer—indolence" and "drowsy noons,/ And evenings steep'd in honied indolence," becomes, as it moves from body into mind and from vagary into passion, the entranced yet vivid introspection that precipitates the greater odes. "The true voice" of Keats's marvelously fertile indolence begins to speak in the "Ode on Melancholy," and at last the rather unpleasantly sprawling satisfaction of the poet in the "Ode on Indolence" matures into the erect, impersonal, complexly symbolic figure of the most significant image in

Keats: the gleaner of "To Autumn," who "dost keep/ Steady thy laden head. . . ."

The "Ode on Melancholy" and "To Autumn" form a kind of frame around the picture of Keats as tragic artist, in the sense that the one sets the precipitating negative conviction and the other answers it positively by accepting and then transmuting the negative; within that frame the other two odes labor toward the positive but stop short. In the "Ode on Melancholy" Keats conducts a tragic initiate through *lacrimae rerum* to a refuge that proves bitterly paradoxical: "Ay, in the very temple of Delight/ Veil'd Melancholy has her sovran shrine." The definition of sadness is acid and hopeless and takes its perverse satisfaction from a kind of heroic vagueness or grandly magnified helplessness at the end of the poem: "His soul shall taste the sadness of her might,/ And be among her cloudy trophies hung." Within the scope of this poem the mood is definitive and perfectly realized; but within the scheme of the "ode-sequence" the mood is inconclusive. The argument is one that had to be cleared away before movement could take place, a brush-burning before the new seeding.

In the "Ode to a Nightingale" Keats continues his waking-dream state of the "Ode on Indolence," but with an important shift of accent and direction. The mood of reverie has matured markedly, grown questing and intense and creative; reverie has become the alembic of the passions and the intellect. And so the real mood of the poem is directed not by Indolence but by Melancholy; like the "Ode on a Grecian Urn" and "To Autumn," the "Ode to a Nightingale" really lives in the climate of tragic despair. Like them, also, it tries to escape from that despair, or to make peace within it. As in "To Autumn," Keats tries to build his vehicle of escape from the furnishings of nature. And if we compare the nature-imagery of the

"Nightingale" with that of the "Ode to Psyche," where there is little irruption of the personal dilemma, we see how strikingly the temper of Keats's introspection has deepened and warmed in the course of working through the linked moods of the spring odes. The grand resolution he reaches in the autumn ode is here only a haunting and beautiful irresolution. But that very irresolution becomes, I believe, this poem's basic theme and the core of its significance in the formation of the poet's tragic view.

Irresolution affects the poem's texture and its structure. The "Ode on Melancholy" dwelt in an area of sad certainty in its confident analysis of absolute despair; this ode, which feels no certainty, only the rich doubt of passionate, salvatory, perfectionist aspiration, is marked by greater looseness of thought, of organization, and of detail. Keats's position in the poem is now much more intimately subjective, and this means that things are seen in softer outlines and sweeter tones, that they are less firmly and rationally controlled. The dramatic condition of the poem is one of interaction, basically of opposition, between the aspiring and the achieving spirit, poet and bird—between "My heart aches" and "thine Happiness." Two motifs are fundamental: the bird's symbolic embodiment of immutable ideality, especially the superhuman power to transcend time and the vale of tears, and the movement of the dramatic line, which rises to a hesitant, imperfect identification in the fourth and fifth stanzas, then slowly collapses to a quiet confession of defeat. Stanza seven sums up the symbolic oppositions of the theme. The poet, involved in a brief ironic illusion of permanence on "this passing night," confronts his mutability in confessing the uniqueness of the bird's transcendent power of speech to "emperor and clown," to the exiled Ruth, to the persons of romantic fable; the beauty makes bearable the fatality.

The "Ode on a Grecian Urn" is an intricately manipulated conceit, beautifully observed and reasoned. The voluble artifact, the urn, is invited to speak its abstract music to the abstracted ear—to "Pipe to the spirit ditties of no tone"—and it speaks, through eloquent concrete images and a gnomic text, sufficient wisdom. In terms of the tragic vision, the movement of the poem is substantially that of the "Ode to a Nightingale": the questing spirit, still trapped in the vale of Melancholy, mining his passionate bemusement in search of succor and release, turns for salvation to the world of created art. He receives comfort and illumination and finally a great abstract insight, but no full salvation. The "Ode on a Grecian Urn" again confirms human life as an order of merely negative tragedy—or pathos; it again confirms high art as a contrasted order of achieved magnificence. Yet the effect of the famous crux of the closing lines is both to amplify and to undercut the "established" themes, and thereby to force a radical shift in our standard despair.

One thing the eloquent urn proposes in its equation of Beauty and Truth, it seems to me, is the further dry-eyed insight that Despair is also Truth. It is the position assumed at the end of the "Ode on Melancholy" and, with complications, at the end of the "Ode to a Nightingale." But when we can call the insight into Despairing Truth an insight into Beauty as well, we have begun to mature beyond pathos into tragedy, and to move toward that point where we stand not annihilated by Truth but reassembled by it. The "Ode on a Grecian Urn" makes a crucial gesture toward the fulfillment of the tragic sense of life. It shows a man driven out of life into thought, out of thought into art, and out of art back into thought. But Keats's decisive motion here has yet to be welcomed into the self, reembodied, and projected beyond the self in an adequately complex and active form; these are the things that take place in the multifoliate image of the last ode.

I feel that the ode "To Autumn," in its deceptive seeming simplicity, is the least understood and the most undervalued of Keats's poems. Most critics have said, in effect, that it is formally the most perfect, thematically the thinnest of the great odes, a technical masterpiece but thoughtless; it is a beautiful landscape but static, mute, without significance beyond its own frame. Allen Tate puts the type-judgment succinctly, and we can borrow that as a sally-port for a new approach to the poet-philosopher Keats had become: "'Ode to Autumn' is a very nearly perfect piece of style but it has little to say."

Middleton Murry wrote of the ode as follows:

> It need not be pointed out with a finger how deeply Shakespearean that perfect poem is—Shakespearean in its rich and opulent serenity of mood, Shakespearean in its lovely and large periodic movement, like the drawing of a deep, full breath. . .It is the perfect and unforced utterance of the truth contained in the magic words: 'Ripeness is all.'

F. R. Leavis' brusque rebuttal to this passage in Murry reconstitutes the usual reading of the poem:

> Such talk is extravagant, and does not further the appreciation of Keats. No one could have found that order of significance in the Ode merely by inspecting the Ode itself. The ripeness with which Keats is concerned is the physical ripeness of autumn, and his genius manifests itself in the sensuous richness with which he renders this in poetry, without the least touch of artistic overripeness.

The lush looseness of the one and the dry concentration of the other are characteristic of the two critics. And while both are right in a way, Murry, rhapsodizing and all, seems to me righter. I feel that he is not extravagant but newly just when he places the ode in the context of Shakespeare and of tragedy, and that that "order of significance" can be found in the ode itself, in its nature and its stature.

My special sense of "To Autumn" is that it is the ode in which the warring extremes of the tragic sense of life are finally reconciled and liberated. Far from having "little to say," it is crowded with audible wisdom, and the chief thing it says is indeed Edgar's "Ripeness is all"; or, to avoid the elementary confusion with the "ripe" season that troubles Mr. Leavis, perhaps Hamlet's "The readiness is all" would serve better. I agree that the ode seems to say little—we do not see its lips move. But poetry can speak in ways other than loud logical discourse. One of these ways of mute eloquence is the speaking drama of imagery.

The first stanza is made up almost entirely of a crowded catalogue of sight images that record the immense fruitfulness of the season by multiplying visions of fullness, heaviness, ripeness—a sensation of fruition now absolute and perfect. But one gradually comes to realize that the images are not so much visual as tactual; the objects seen are more importantly felt, and this empathic effect is carried by the strikingly simple, active, vigorous verbs of touch and pressure: "load," "bless," "bend," "fill," "swell," "plump," "set budding," and "o'er-brimmed."

In stanza two the personification of Autumn has become intimate and detailed, and the form of the gleaner has become a specific figure of focus. Keats sets that figure in a sequence of stylized offices that are really attitudes or postures more than they are actions, forming a striking and very subtle combination of understated dramatic moods. The moods are passive—"careless," "steady," "patient"—suspended and fixed while half-complete. The image-sense is again notably empathic, combining sensations of sight, smell, touch, taste; but the stanza's impression is defined almost more significantly by the missing sense, sound: an interesting and complex soundlessness renders, silently, the coordinating mood of dreamy suspension.

The closing stanza is dominated by that sense that was withheld in stanza two. The resumption here, after the silence, of the droning hum of autumnal noises reminds one of the behavior of the autumn locust's cry—that slightly syncopated, slightly off-key song, rising to its crescendo, stopping sharp off, beginning again; he appears in person in the "hedge-crickets" of the ninth line. At any rate, almost all the images here are auditory ones; we may therefore be struck first by the shift, since the first stanza, in the sound of the verse, the shift to a kind of thin minor that is carried by the multiplication of short *i* and *e* sounds. Hearing the developed contrast to the confident, robust roundness of sound in stanza one offers an elementary insight into the poem; if that leads us to a closer look at the images of the third stanza in order to see by what means other than sound the effect is achieved, we have begun our first real penetration.

For if we really scrutinize those images, we see that they fall into an elaborate pattern of intentional equivocation. Virtually every image or pair of images forms a paradox, an oxymoron: the images make two gestures, promising and threatening; celebrate two moods, joyful and sorrowful; look in two directions, backward to summer, forward to winter, backward to life, forward to death. The opposition that is set under way by the response of "thy music" to the "songs of Spring" is carried out in beautiful and explicit detail in the images that follow. First the "barred clouds" reach all the way back to the opening stanza to qualify softly its "maturing sun" and "warm days." Then, within the frame of the third stanza alone, "bloom" is counterposed to "dying"; "stubble" is opposed to "rosy." In line five "wailful" and "mourn" undercut and darkly color our notions of a "choir" as a positive voice of joy or praise or a merely neutral voice of solemnity. In line six does Keats choose "sallows" for its color connotations instead of the less evocative "willows"? Clearly, at any rate, "borne aloft" is counterposed to "sinking" as "lives" is to "dies." The lambs now "full-grown" deny their spring; their "bleat" is their standard cry, but our extra sense of it is sad and pathetic. The hedge-crickets are the stanza's only largely neutral image; but even that neutrality is conditioned by their association with the passing season and so with evanescence. The two bird images that complete the poem round out the oxymoronic complex: the song of the red-breast is reduced to a "treble soft"; and the swallows' "twitter" is plaintive, emaciated, anticipatory—portentous, as is their very "gathering."

Significantly, the only other place in which Keats uses this elaborate pattern of paradox is in the "Cave of Quietude" passage in *Endymion*, his first embodiment of tragic reconciliation. We cannot escape its presence here at the end of the ode "To Autumn," and it must drive us back to review the first two stanzas and ask whether the paradox is everywhere in the poem and what force it has in the total meaning. Then we realise at last that the oxymoron was subtly anticipated from the beginning by Keats's piecemeal assembly of a single coordinating metaphor: the sense of the season as a beautiful but fatally fragile equilibrium. The rich configuration of absolute fullness that originally dominates the ode "To Autumn" is itself oxymoronic: perfect fulfillment can only portend decay. The year's harvest is the year's continental divide; the end of its triumph and the beginning of its defeat. With this light borrowed from the closing stanza, we can begin to uncover the long sequence of explicit signal images that have pointed at the poem's theme from the beginning.

In addition to the generic threat of decay in fruition, we

now sense the whispered menace of "they think warm days will never cease" and the dark ambiguities of "o'er-brimmed" and "clammy cells." In the second stanza these impressions crowd upon us: in all the soundless, patient passivity of the personified figure; in all the ramified images of "hook" and harvest; in the narcotic somnolence of the heavy sweetness of odors; in all the multiplied finalities of sound and image. Reflect for a moment, in this connection, on the almost inexhaustible connotativeness of lines like these:

> Or by a cyder-press, with patient look,
> Thou watchest the last oozings hours by hours.

But all these data, all these impressions, are miraculously caught up in the great simple image of the gleaner who "dost keep/ Steady thy laden head across a brook." In that figure, walking level, gliding, fulfilled, calmly toward the death of the year, we have the embodiment of the tragic sense of life: what she carries on her head in serene balance is the burden of the Mystery; where she walks is the high table land of Keats's full maturity of spirit and of art.

I have tried to show the complex sources of the poem's effect; but the effect itself is not complicated. That in a way is the heart of the matter—the simple oneness that results from all the complication. This special poised peace is the theme of the poem; it is what the poem exists to say and it says it by mood and tone and by those brilliantly passive images of the gleaner; we do have to keep coming back to those. What they dramatize is something like catharsis—all passion not spent but reconciled, sublimated, held in philosophical equipoise. The poem says these things within the scheme of the odes as a whole and also within its own proper boundaries. If we think of the odes as a sequence, this ode is their proper terminus in dynamic peace.

Thematically it is immeasurably richer than it has been held to be. That the ode is a "nature poem," as is so often said, is true only in a kindergarten sense. Far from ignoring the conventional mythic and poetic associations of autumn, as some say Keats has done, he exploits exactly that fullest conventional significance with naked originality.

Murry was quite right when he called this a perfect poem; it is one of the species that defines the genus. It is poetry of, the order that Keats called "great & unobtrusive." It is the quality of these odes that makes one more and more certain that Keats is the poet from the nineteenth century who is to satisfy our notions of the wholly valuable, the near ancestor for whom we feel most grateful, the one who best meets the mendicant eye asking passion and grace, susceptibility and manliness, news of art and life.

NOTES

[1] See also Lionel Trilling's splendid essay, "The Poet as Hero: Keats in His Letters," in *The Opposing Self* (New York, 1955).

[2] All reference to Keats's letters are from Hyder Edward Rollins, ed., *The Letters of John Keats, 1814-1821,* 2 vols. (Cambridge: Harvard University Press, 1958) and are reprinted by permission of the publisher and of the President and Fellows of Harvard College. I have preserved Keats's idiosyncrasies of spelling and punctuation except where it was tyographically too cumbersome to do so.

Leviathan Is the Text

IV

Of the texts D. H. Lawrence examines in *Studies in Classic American Literature*, the one that strikes him dumb is *Moby Dick*. "When Leviathan is the text," as Melville says, "the case is altered." Lawrence can only stare and babble. He is dealing with the masterwork of our fiction and one of the world's great books. After 1851 all the men working in those ideal garrets at The Great American Novel were wasting their time: Melville had done the job. In Longinean terms, *Moby Dick* is the first (and perhaps the last) instance of the American "sublime." *The Scarlet Letter* is more perfect, but it is a great deal smaller. *Moby Dick* is great because it triumphs in a moral and aesthetic enterprise of foolhardy magnitude.

The grandeur and beauty of the novel rise above disabilities of some seriousness. A good Christian will find it morally dubious, a strict logician can point to inconsistencies, a classical taste will gag on its rhetoric. At the technical level, the narrative-dramatic method presents a baffling critical problem. The difficulty does not lie in the interspersed cetological matter: that grows straight out of the central business of the novel, forms a bold fugal pattern with the narrative, and in itself stands among the great examples of expository prose in English. It is Melville's management of his persona Ishmael that we are tempted to call a crudity. He seems a bit dim and thin to carry the weighty positive side of Melville's theme. But when Leviathan is the text, the case is altered. The faults are the faults of the Colossus, and in the total figure they do not come to much. They are a remnant awkwardness in the sweepingly generous gesture, the prodigal act, that is the writing of this book.

This wonderful amplitude, of meaning and of force, is what I hope to get at by means of a review of the tragical argument of *Moby Dick*. For the novel is not less than a total metaphor of human life defined as tragedy. Newton Arvin was surely right when he said that the structure and the texture of the novel bring it closer in form to the heroic poem than to tragedy. But though *Moby Dick* is not a tragedy, it is nonetheless tragic. Its "vision" is tragic, as Richard Sewall says in the best of the attempts to define this quality in the book, and what it looks out on is tragedy, the human contest with, and destruction by, the enigmatic powers. We are unjust to the novel unless we relax the Aristotelian strictures and call it tragic; and we do no harm thereby to the primary form, the tragic drama. It is just those qualities that dissuaded Arvin from calling *Moby Dick* a tragedy—its being "large, free, loose, spacious, and open"—that express Melville's mind and spirit, the special generosity of his tragic vision. It matters that the work *Moby Dick* calls most often to mind is *King Lear*, most cosmic of tragedies. The meaning world of the tragic narrative is what I wish to rehearse, the voyage as a fully inclusive trope of human experience.

We feel this seriousness and this inclusiveness in the very first motions of the book, even in points anterior to the action—in the dedication to Nathaniel Hawthorne, for instance, "in token of my admiration for his genius"; in the very first bit of the epigraphic matter, the "Etymology," "supplied by a late consumptive usher to a grammar school":

> ... ever dusting his old lexicons and grammars, with a queer handkerchief, mockingly embellished with all the gay flags of all the known nations of the world. He loved to dust his old grammars; it somehow mildly reminded him of his mortality.

Among the prefatory "Extracts," the example of the little

sea-gudgeon who retires into the whale's mouth "in great security, and there sleeps" anticipates an important subsidiary metaphor, to be developed in the voyage.

Then the beautiful little first chapter, dominantly wry-comic like most of the first main movement of the novel, is strongly touched by the dreamy mysteriousness that is one of the book's essences, one of the counterpointed moods that compose the difficult harmony of the human spirit. Melville fixes the relationship of his medium and his motive in a swift phrase: ". . .meditation and water are wedded forever." Ishmael sees the water-bound Manhattanites as a race of ruminants: "Posted like silent sentinels all around the town, stand thousands upon thousands of mortal men fixed in ocean reveries." Water, we are told, holds "the image of the ungraspable phantom of life." In this first chapter we learn fundamental things about Ishmael's reading of the world, and about his motive. It is a world inherited from the "two orchard thieves," where "head winds are far more prevalent than winds from astern," and where "the universal thump is passed round." Ishmael, we see already, is a whole-minded young man, aware of the malign cast of experience, but not blind to the benign side, and with good humor ready for either—"since it is but well to be on friendly terms with all the inmates of the place one lodges in." And we learn at once of the impetus and the emblem of Ishmael's own quest, the form "the ungraspable phantom of life" is to assume here, "the overwhelming idea of the great whale himself," the "portentous and mysterious monster" in his most portentous and mysterious shape, "one grand hooded phantom, like a snow hill in the air."

Most of this first movement of the novel, down to that "short, cold Christmas" when the crew of the Pequod "gave three heavy-hearted cheers, and blindly plunged like fate into the lone Atlantic," is easy and open-hearted in feeling, divided between Ishmael's engagingly slow and naive approach to the business of whaling and the charming "hearts' honeymoon" of the staunch new friends, the Christian Ishmael and the pagan Queequeg, or "George Washington cannibalistically developed." But in that relationship ("I felt a melting in me. No more my splintered heart and maddened hand were turned against the wolfish world. This soothing savage had redeemed it") and in other motions of the early chapters, central metaphors of the voyage begin to work. The three chapters devoted to Father Mapple, his New Bedford chapel, and his sermon thicken the texture notably. While a sleet storm howls outside, Ishmael sits among the marble tablets that memorialize the whalemen lost at sea, "placelessly perished without a grave," and thinks of the terrors of death and of the astonishing fact that ". . .Faith, like a jackal, feeds among the tombs, and even from these dead doubts she gathers her most vital hope." Father Mapple preaches on the text of Jonah and the whale—"Beloved shipmates, clinch the last verse of the first chapter of Jonah"—and takes from it what he calls a "two-stranded lesson." The first strand is Miltonic and applies ultimately to Ahab: "And if we obey God, we must disobey ourselves. . . ." The second strand applies to the priest and inferentially to Melville and Ishmael as witnesses and narrators of God's world, of the exempla of man's experience in the hands of God:

> Woe to him who seeks to pour oil upon the waters when God has brewed them into a gale! Woe to him who seeks to please rather than to appal!. . .Woe to him who would not be true, even though to be false were salvation! Yea, woe to him who, as the great Pilot Paul has it, while preaching to others is himself a castaway!

It is strenuous yet devious doctrine, enjoining both

independence and humility, and qualifying faith with both an inner rationalism and a fact-facing pessimism. The total doctrine indeed may be said to present a third "strand," an insistent relativism vital to the argument of the novel to come.

But the furnishing and gestures of the scene are emblematic, too. That encompassing spirituality which is the climate of *Moby Dick*, whatever violence may be done to the spirit in the progress of the action, is prefigured in Ishmael's reflection on the image of the old mariner-priest in his whimsical nautical pulpit:

> What could be more full of meaning? — for the pulpit is ever this earth's foremost part; all the rest comes in its rear; the pulpit leads the world. From thence it is the storm of God's quick wrath is first descried, and the bow must bear the earliest brunt. From thence it is the God of breezes fair or foul is first invoked for favorable winds. Yes, the world's a ship on its passage out, and not a voyage complete; and the pulpit is its prow.

The metaphor of life as a moral voyage, and one open-ended and dynamic, is given us there; and two other obsessive metaphors of the special voyage that is *Moby Dick* are also shadowed forth in this scene. The metaphor of withdrawal, salutary for defense and reflection, begins here when Father Mapple pulls up his rope ladder to isolate himself in his pulpit, "impregnable in his little Quebec." Ishmael feels that the act "signifies his spiritual withdrawal," "replenished with the meat and wine of the word," in a "self-containing stronghold—a lofty Ehrenbreitstein, with a perennial well of water within the walls." And the haunting group of images that compose what I should call the metaphor of profundity are anticipated in the sermon scene by the way in which Melville describes Father Mapple's act of prayer before and after his sermon: "...a prayer so deeply devout that he seemed kneeling and praying at the bottom of the sea."

The chapter on "The Ship," though still conducted in the comic-ironic hyperbole characteristic of the early novel, also looks ahead to later tragic concerns. The Pequod is presented as a special ship, special in symbolic ways. She personifies the life she will convey. She is ancient and universal. In a single paragraph, Melville draws figures from England, France, Germany, Scandinavia, Siberia, Tartary, Ethiopia, and Japan to suggest her world-wide origins and experience. And she participates in, is penetrated by, the whale—her quarry and her structural element. "She was a thing of trophies. A cannibal of a craft, tricking herself forth in the chased bones of her enemies." Her hempen lines run over sheaves of whale bone and are fastened to pins of sperm whale teeth; her tiller is carved from a whale's lower jaw. "A noble craft, but somehow a most melancholy!" is Ishmael's impression; and then he generalizes, "All noble things are touched with that." Later in the same chapter Melville applies the association of nobility and melancholy to character, as, speaking now of the type of the world-roving Nantucket Quaker, he begins in the first swelling of his grand heroic rhetoric to prepare a case for Ahab as a person of tragic fable:

> And when these things unite in a man of greatly superior natural force, with a globular brain and a ponderous heart; who has also by the stillness and seclusion of many long night-watches in the remotest waters, and beneath constellations never seen here at the north, been led to think untraditionally and independently; receiving all nature's sweet or savage impressions fresh from her own virgin voluntary and confiding breast, and thereby chiefly. . .to learn a bold and nervous lofty language — that man makes one in a whole nation's census — a mighty pageant creature, formed for noble tragedies. Nor will it at all detract from him, dramatically regarded, if either by birth or other circumstances, he have what seems a half wilful over-ruling morbidness

at the bottom of his nature. For all men tragically great are made so through a certain morbidness.

Melville knows that only a great language can give the stature of tragedy to his hero and his action. He knows, as he says later, that in one sense he is dealing only with "an old whale-hunter"; he knows equally that he has equipped and surrounded his hero from the "kingly commons" with a bold and nervous lofty language.

Though the book deepens under Melville's hand as it moves through its action, it works at its crucial concerns from the first page. Meanwhile, the first movement finds its private coda, and the metaphors an early summation, in the superb little chapter in which Ishmael apostrophizes Bulkington, the new-landed mariner whose brawn and introspective dignity he had admired in New Bedford and who now abruptly reappears, as if "the land seemed scorching to his feet," at the helm of the Pequod. Melville offers the "six-inch chapter" as epitaph to the man's heroism, a sign for "the stoneless grave of Bulkington." His reembarkation is the restlessness of an insatiable spirit, and Melville's trope for that is the voyaging act itself. What evolves is one of the controlling metaphors of the novel as a whole. There will be good and bad conduct on the voyage, and ultimate disaster for all but Ishmael. But the good and the bad are alike superior to the withholding, that abnegation or disengagement for which the land, "the turnpike earth," stands here:

> Know ye, now, Bulkington? Glimpses do ye seem to see of that mortally intolerable truth; that all deep, earnest thinking is but the intrepid effort of the soul to keep the open independence of her sea; while the wildest winds of heaven and earth conspire to cast her on the treacherous, slavish shore?
>
> But as in landlessness alone resides the highest truth, shoreless, indefinite as God — so, better is it to perish in that howling infinite,

than be ingloriously dashed upon the lee, even if that were safety! For worm-like, then, oh! who would craven crawl to land! Terrors of the terrible! is all this agony so vain? Take heart, take heart, O Bulkington! Bear thee grimly, demigod! Up from the spray of thy ocean-perishing — straight up, leaps thy apotheosis!

II

But *Moby Dick* becomes fully itself when the prow of the Pequod plunges into the lone Atlantic. Thenceforth we follow her "circumnavigating wake." The action is extensive, outmoving, flung out toward the appointment with the great white whale in a fated space-time. At one level the voyage is sheer adventure; at another, a commercial enterprise, the pursuit of a valuable commodity; at another it is therapy, treatment for a besetting landlocked depression; at another, the exposition of a cetological education; at another, the prosecution of a fantastic outrage and revenge. In Melville's governing intelligence it is all these things and yet another: a symbolical exploration of all the mysterious seas of life, the pursuit and confrontation of the "ungraspable phantom," the shape and meaning of experience itself. The book surely composes one of the grandest and most intricate harmonies in the history of art, one of the signal achievements of the penetrating and synthesizing imagination, of what Coleridge resonantly calls the "esemplastic" power of the mind. Melville controls his enterprise by great dramatizing discipline—by creation of events which are true as actions and as symbols, giving ideas a local habitation and a name; and by his own bold and nervous lofty language, which is at once the form and the integument of the action.

Aristotle says that "the greatest thing by far is to be a master of metaphor"; Melville is one of the masters of metaphor, and in the grand, double, Shakespearean way: of metaphor as a small illuminating grammatical member; and of action as metaphor—general action and particular actions which stand forth as "meaning": analogical embodiments, ideas incarnated. Melville's metaphors in this latter sense, to take at once an artificially lofty and abstract view of them, make a complex and significant pattern—lines of extension and profundity, long horizontals and deep verticals.

His conception of the crew of the Pequod has the stiffness and geometricity of allegory; but its execution has the roundness and fluency of great symbolism. The created figures move before the eye with the heightened significance of the great romantic fictions. Moving the allegory and giving it life is Melville's heartbroken humanism, his sense of man as grand and absurd, doomed and pathetically imposing, in the long run a creature who infinitely matters. "Seat thyself sultanically among the moons of Saturn," he suggests toward the end of the novel, "and take high abstracted man alone; and he seems a wonder, a grandeur, and a woe." Earlier, anticipating "the fall of valor in the soul" of Starbuck, he speaks his defensive love of the race:

> Men may seem detestable as joint stock-companies and nations; knaves, fools, and murderers there may be; men may have mean and meagre faces; but man, in the ideal, is so noble and so sparkling, such a grand and glowing creature, that over any ignominious blemish in him all his fellows should run to throw their costliest robes.

Melville is perfectly aware that it is to "meanest mariners, and renegades and castaways" that he is to "ascribe high qualities, though dark; weave round them tragic graces. . . ." But it is those same commons, at their kingly best, who produce the "selectest champions."

The metaphor of the crew as a whole moves both horizontally and vertically. Melville could scarcely be franker about his horizontal figure. He compounds his crew by picking men at pointed intervals from a line rolled out about the globe, men of all creeds and colors, and groups them in one of his memorable single metaphors:

> ...federated along one keel, what a set those Isolatoes were! An Anacharsis Clootz delegation from all the isles of the sea, and all the ends of the earth, accompanying Old Ahab in the Pequod to lay the world's grievances before that bar from which not very many of them ever came back.

It is the race itself that undertakes this voyage to the mysterious beckoning and threatening throne of God. But the crew is universalized in the vertical metaphor as well, in a hierarchical cross-cutting of the race on a scale of types of personality and capacity. In the governing emblematical structure of the novel, Melville draws a nearly exact equation between a man's function and his worth, arranging the main body of the crew under Ahab in a precise descending order. He makes the relationship explicit again and again, as when Ahab as "Pope" addresses the mates as "my sweet cardinals"; or in the chapter on "The Cabin Table," where the dining order descends from the "sultan" or "Grand Turk" Ahab, through the mates as first, second and third "Emir," to "those inferior fellows the harpooneers." In the same feudalistic way, Ahab commands the parent vessel and the whole crew, while each of the mates as "knight" commands a small whale boat, a harpooneer as "squire," and a subsidiary crew of oarsmen.

It is important to see why the mates are subordinated, and to what they are inadequate. Melville develops their typological weaknesses in a thoroughly realistic way. We recognize them as human familiars. Stubb, for example, to adapt Fielding's phrase, is "not only alive, but hath been so these four thousand years." The trouble with them all is that they are too merely men. Melville sums up the hierarchy of the crew and reduces the complex inadequacy of each of the mates to a phrase at the end of the chapter, "Moby Dick":

> Here, then, was this grey-headed, ungodly old man, chasing with curses a Job's whale round the world, at the head of a crew, too, chiefly made up of mongrel renegades. . .morally enfeebled also, by the incompetence of mere unaided virtue or right-mindedness in Starbuck, the invulnerable jollity of indifference and recklessness in Stubb, and the pervading mediocrity in Flask.

Briefly then they are disqualified by not being Ahabs. Certainly Starbuck, and probably Stubb, would qualify to lead an ordinary whaling voyage. But this is an extraordinary voyage after a peculiar whale. The voyage is in fact the exteriorizing of a moral absolute: to conceive and conduct such a totality needs an Ahab.

Certain figures, Ahab and Ishmael among them, stand in a special oblique relationship to the hierarchy conceived as a normal human order. The little black cabin-boy Pip, who jumps from the whale boat in his great fear and goes mad when he is abandoned for hours in the heartless hurry of the chase, moves at the vague bottom of the scale. He plays the Fool to Ahab's Lear, and in the novel as in the play a range of special pathos and irony enters the tragic action in the union of the highest and the lowest men in a common fate and feeling. Like Ahab in *his* madness (and Lear and the Fool in theirs), Pip has peculiar powers and insights, though different from Ahab's. They come to him through his terrible experience of abandonment in the vacant universe of the ocean. Melville 'presents the case in the beautiful chapter of "The Castaway":

> The sea had jeeringly kept his finite body up, but drowned the infinite of his soul. Not drowned entirely, though. Rather carried down alive to wondrous depths, where strange shapes of the unwarped primal world glided to and fro before his passive eyes; and the miser-merman, Wisdom, revealed his hoarded heaps; and among the joyous, heartless, ever-juvenile eternities, Pip saw the multitudinous, God-omnipresent, coral insects, that out of the firmament of waters heaved the colossal orbs. He saw God's foot upon the treadle of the loom, and spoke it; and therefore his shipmates called him mad. So man's insanity is heaven's sense; and wandering from all mortal reason, man comes at last to that celestial thought, which, to reason, is absurd and frantic; and weal or woe, feels then uncompromised, indifferent as his God.

In that mystical passage, two of Melville's primary metaphors, that of profound descent and that of the cosmic loom, come together to express the miraculous spiritualization of Pip.

For a different reason, Ahab's boat's crew of Parsees also stand apart. Significantly, their habitation on the ship is a sort of chthonic area in the hold. They are fire-worshippers, marked by a special pagan diabolism, an active and absolute anti-Christianity, and we have to see them as creatures of Ahab's perverted moral imagination and extensions of his frenzied will. But Ahab's particularity and Ishmael's must be reviewed at greater length.

III

Critics have likened Ahab to Lucifer, Job, Prometheus, Faust, Lear, and those images suggest his species without,

somehow, defining his genus. He is of the type of the great
hero-villains, certainly, but in the long run he is himself only, a
great perverted nature, the perfection of his own type. ". . .he's
Ahab, boy," Peleg tells Ishmael before the captain of the
Pequod has ever appeared; and at the end of the book, after the
white whale has been met and as the catastrophe approaches,
Ahab shouts to the mates, "Starbuck is Stubb reversed, and
Stubb is Starbuck; and ye two are all mankind; and Ahab stands
alone among the millions of the peopled earth, nor gods nor
men his neighbors!" Ahab is never incredible as a mere man, yet
he is a grand and terrible being. If "all outward majestical
trappings and housings" are denied to a "poor old whale-hunter
like him," the inward trappings and housings are majestical
enough to make him the greatest of the folk-heroes of tragedy.
Ahab is a genius, a twisted giant of the mind, of terrific power
and passion; his are "a globular brain and a ponderous heart,"
which is to say more than 'round and heavy.' Peleg's description
is precise: "He's a grand, ungodly, godlike man, Captain Ahab."
In his practical function he is incomparable: ". . .a Khan of the
plank, and a king of the sea, and a great lord of Leviathans was
Ahab." He is superbly superior to every natural crisis his ship
meets, and fabricates crises of his own for the sheer sultanic
pleasure of exercizing his will and his skill: "Ahab is lord over
the level loadstone"; "I crush the quadrant, the thunder turns the
needles, and now the mad sea parts the log-line. But Ahab can
mend all." But like his blacksmith Perth, Ahab can smooth any
seam or dent but one, and that is the seam of his own ribbed
brow, the ensign of his immitigable woe: that, as he says, "has
worked down into the bone of my skull."

   To suggest the magisterial power of his "mighty pageant
creature" Melville is repeatedly led to imperial epithets—King,

Emperor, Khan, Czar, Grand Turk, Pope, Sultan. The analogies signify his lofty pride and isolation as well as his power. "Who's over me?" he demands. Ahab's "sultanism" takes the form, on board the Pequod, of absolute tyranny, "an irresistible dictatorship." Such tyranny was traditional in the whale fishery; but as always *Moby Dick* presents the perfection of the form, an evil and fascinating possession of the souls of men. Hawthorne suggests that that sort of possession, the usurpation of another's soul, is the unforgivable sin. But I do not think that is the way Melville sees Ahab primarily; his crime is directed against himself, and lies in his perversion of his own nature, as representative of man's nature at its most splendid. That pervertedness is suggested by Pip's description, "that anaconda of an old man." But the truest phrase is Starbuck's vague and simple, "Horrible old man!" for that shows how the perversion transpires within human limits, keeps the form of man's mind and body, is worked by his own will. Ahab is a bad *man*.

He is so mighty and real that we must fear him; but astonishingly neither we nor anyone on board the Pequod can hate him. We pity, fear, and admire him because of the dreadful things he has done to his human nature, but also because his mad motive is in some sense ours. In his wounding and his huge outrage at the design of things, we recognize the racial alienation, the family loneliness. We witness with awe his refusal to accept his limited human nature, his definition by the universe. His obsession is fatal and wrong, but it is noble. And though Melville shows us relatively little of Ahab's softer, sweeter side, we see enough to agree easily with Peleg that "stricken, blasted, if he be, Ahab has his humanities!"

Ahab's loneliness is both pitiable and imposing. Melville expresses it in a rugged and barbarous conceit:

He lived in the world, as the last of the Grisly Bears lived in settled Missouri. And as when Spring and Summer has departed, that wild Logan of the woods, burying himself in the hollow of a tree, lived out the winter there, sucking his own paws, so, in his inclement, howling old age, Ahab's soul, shut up in the caved trunk of his body, there fed upon the sullen paws of its gloom!

He has cast off from the race, and typically he both glories in and is tortured by his isolation. He has willed his alienation, but he does not wholly control it: it is a property of his nature, his imprisoning greatness of mind and passion. In part, Ahab is alone because he towers. But he is an immensity who is still a man, an intensification and extravagance of human traits and powers. Thus Melville's hero, in his size and sweep, stands at the center of his cosmical metaphor, the voyage as a total trope of experience. And by standing so monumentally he becomes one of the book's prime metaphors of vertical extension. His flesh as bound to earth is thoroughly real and efficient ("all rib and keel was solid Ahab"), but his insatiable spirit stretches high above the normal element and probes profoundly beneath it. " 'Mark ye, be forewarned,' " Peleg cautions Ishmael,

'Ahab's above the common; Ahab's been in colleges, as well as 'mong the cannibals; been used to deeper wonders than the waves; fixed his lance in mightier, stranger foes than whales.'

Ahab is a great man who has spent a long life asking the most ultimate and exasperated questions of the universe, and who is finally driven mad by the answers he thinks he has heard. It is of this ruthless out-reaching speculation of mind that Ishmael is thinking when he says, "Oh, Ahab! what shall be grand in thee, it must needs be plucked at from the skies, and dived for in the deep, and featured in the unbodied air!"

Ahab's profundity, his "larger, darker, deeper part," is expressed in a figure one feels haunting Melville's own deepest feeling as well as his deepest literary memory:

> Winding far down from within the very heart of this spiked Hotel de
> Cluny where we here stand — however grand and wonderful, now quit
> it; — and take your way, ye nobler, sadder souls, to those vast Roman
> halls of Thermes; where far beneath the fantastic towers of man's
> upper earth, his root of grandeur, his whole awful essence sits in
> bearded state; an antique buried beneath antiquities, and throned on
> torsoes! So with a broken throne, the great gods mock that captive
> king; so like a Caryatid, he patient sits, upholding on his frozen brow
> the piled entablatures of ages. Wind ye down there, ye prouder, sadder
> souls! question that proud, sad king! A family likeness! aye, he did
> beget ye, ye young exiled royalties; and from your grim sire only will
> the old State-secret come.

One recalls the classical, the Dantean, and the Miltonic
underworlds, and perhaps the whole Romantic fascination with
fallen Rome; I am most intimately reminded of Keats's
Hyperion. The effect, at any rate, is an immense abstraction of
the human creature, as a Titan overmastered by gods, his history
a heaping of defeat, brooding forevermore on his lost estate. The
image shows us for what we must be grateful to Ahab, while we
pity and fear him: he has thought and felt for his kind in
terms of its inclusive destiny. He is a race hero—"aye, he did
beget ye. . . ." He is man at his grandest and most erroneous:
only so great a man can be so heroically wrong.

The image of man as fallen Titan, prisoner of divine insult,
homesick for a fantastic lost patrimony, frantic to destroy the
gods if he cannot be one of them, goes far to define Ahab's
insanity. Of course Ahab's is a monomania, he is but mad north-
northwest; and so he continues to qualify as tragic hero. Melville
puts the case in plain diagrammatic terms: "If such a furious trope
may stand," he says, "his special lunacy stormed his general
sanity, and carried it, and turned all its concentrated cannon
upon its own mad mark. . . ." Captain Peleg is helpful again:
" 'In fact, he ain't sick; but no, he isn't well either!' " Ahab's

bodily wound is of course his "reaped away" leg, his "dismasting" by Moby Dick when he had snatched the line-knife from his smashed boat and attacked, "blindly seeking with a six-inch blade to reach the fathom-deep life of the whale"; and his subsequent wound on shore when his whale-ivory leg had broken under him and stabbed his groin. But Melville makes it plain that the real wound was in Ahab's mind and soul. In his long recovery from his first wound on the homeward voyage, "Ahab and anguish lay stretched together in one hammock," and then "his torn body and gashed soul bled into one another; and so interfusing, made him mad." Ahab's mind then made two immense and fatal leaps, and one cannot finally say whether they are cause or effect of his madness. He concluded that the whale's attack was purposeful, and that it was motivated by a supernatural animosity to himself of which the white whale was agent and emblem:

> The White Whale swam before him as the monomaniac incarnation of all those malicious agencies which some deep men feel eating in them, till they are left living on with half a heart and half a lung. That intangible malignity which has been from the beginning; to whose dominion even the modern Christians ascribe one-half of the worlds; which the ancient Ophites of the east reverenced in their statue devil; – Ahab did not fall down and worship it like them; but deliriously transferring its idea to the abhorred White Whale, he pitted himself, all mutilated, against it. All that most maddens and torments; all that stirs up the lees of things; all truth with malice in it; all that cracks the sinews and cakes the brain; all the subtle demonisms of life and thought, all evil, to crazy Ahab, were visibly personified, and made practically assailable in Moby Dick. He piled upon the whale's white hump the sum of all the rage and hate felt by his whole race from Adam down; and then, as if his chest had been a mortar, he burst his hot heart's shell upon it.

Ahab's sinful error lies in the egoism of these assumptions, the aggrandizement of self that makes it possible to think he

matters this much in the scheme of things, and his presumption
of the right to read the mind of God. Starbuck calls the quest
a blasphemy: " 'Vengeance on a dumb brute! ...that simply
smote thee from blindest instinct!' " We can only agree. Ahab's
mind is gripped by a kind of Manichaeanism, or a blasphemous
hypertrophy of Calvinist absolutism, which turns God and man
into irreconcilable foes. Of the whale he says, " 'I see in him
outrageous strength, with an inscrutable malice sinewing it.' "
But the egoism and the blasphemy are imposing because they
are racial as well as personal: Ahab suffers, speaks, and acts for all
of us; and because they are the extravagance of a tragic truth, the
reality of human defeat and destruction, "that intangible malignity that has been from the beginning."

Still, when Ahab says, " 'That inscrutable thing is chiefly
what I hate,' " he gives us the clue to the deadly subversion of
his mind and soul. Hatred has taken over his whole being, and in
becoming that single implacable essence he has ceased to
function in the tension of warring and harmonizing urges that is
ordinary human nature. Surely this is the basic iconography of
Ahab's mysterious "birthmark," the "slender rod-like mark,
lividly whitish," which reminds Ishmael of a lightning scar on
the trunk of a great tree, and which the old second-sighted
Manxman ("a man from Man") believed marked him "from
crown to sole." With his birthmark and his lost leg, Ahab is a
riven and dismembered creature, not a whole man. In his
Manichaean absolutism, "dark Ahab" has lost half his capacity to
feel flexibly, to enjoy, to love. Ishmael calls it a malignancy, and
he is right: Ahab's hate is cancerous within him, displacing, as it
swells, the health of his mind and heart. Thus when he stumps
the deck on his leg of flesh and his leg of ivory, we are meant
to see the calcification of one half of his nature: "On life and
death this old man walked." But he is imposing, God knows,

and when Ishmael sees him first he feels "an infinity of firmest fortitude, a determinate, unsurrenderable wilfulness, in the fixed and fearless forward dedication of that glance." And he is infinitely moving in his great suffering and sadness: "...moody stricken Ahab stood...with a crucifixion in his face; in all the nameless regal overbearing dignity of some mighty woe." The woe is not less touching because it is mad: it is, as I say, the extravagance of a generic human woe. In its extravagance, it leads us by contrast to Ishmael.

IV

Ishmael's place in the hierarchy of the crew and in the meanings of the voyage is obviously the most special after Ahab's. He stands low in the crew, virtually an anonymity among them, yet Melville chooses him to survive the Pequod's catastrophe: " 'And I only am escaped alone to tell thee.' " His escape is in one sense sheer accident; in another sense mere technical necessity; yet in such an elaborately symbolic structure the event must mean something that we need to understand. Doubtless it matters symbolically, for example, that he is saved temporarily by Queequeg's whimsical coffin adapted as a life-buoy, and finally by the "devious-cruising Rachel" in search of her captain's lost son. Ishmael's thematic function in the novel is rich and comprehensible; but he remains an imperfect porter of his load. What we can see of him is perfectly adequate to his practical function, and we can accept his symbolic force if we can agree to the fiction that his is the perceiving and speaking intelligence in the novel. But Melville ventriloquizes so long and so beautifully through his narrative mask that Ishmael the man keeps fading out as a visible presence in the action.

The novel is the dramatic record of a process of exposure and instruction that adds up to an education. If it is Ishmael who says, "A whale ship was my Yale College and my Harvard," then the voyage of the Pequod conducts his apprenticeship in the mystery of men and their world, their work and their destiny. Certainly the speaker of the last chapters is not the speaker of the first chapters; but why should he be? He has changed because he has learned, as he has followed the Pequod's "circumnavigating wake." The technical problem may rest only on the fact that Melville does not show us enough of Ishmael in the flesh; the voice remains too disembodied. Ishmael's is a puny nature at no point; but it is still not easy to account for the powers that are meant to qualify him to understand, and to survive, the catastrophic action that is the voyage.

To put the case summarily at once, what saves Ishmael is the wholeness of his humanity. Compared to the "mighty pageant creature" Ahab, Ishmael is a mediocrity. That he is not, and cannot be, the hero of the main action helps to define the action as true tragedy. He is not even a representative of the "kingly commons," as Melville means that term. He goes too quietly about the matter of living to let us suspect he is the stuff of heroes. In the great quest of Ahab's revenge Ishmael is fairly passive and anonymous. But more than one white whale is being sought here, and for different motives. Melville is pushing a less noisy, more implicit quest—for the truth of the nature of things. In his quiet way, Ishmael is the hero of that corollary quest. Emerson might have seen in him Man Thinking. He makes use of the Pequod, and even of Ahab, as he seeks the illumination of his mind and heart. Time and experience complicate his vision, but they do not sour or muddy it. The process is the refining of a normal nature, as Ahab's is the hypertrophy of a great flawed or partial nature.

Important components of Ishmael's wholeness show themselves very early in the novel. At the end of the first chapter, for example, we find him saying, "Not ignoring what is good, I am quick to perceive a horror, and could still be social with it—would they let me—since it is but well to be on friendly terms with all the inmates of the place one lodges in." There is a jejune quality in Ishmael's early dyspepsia; but he himself recognizes the mannerism and relative shallowness of his sadness. The voyage will both enlarge and purify it. Three traits strike one in Ishmael's thought in its early stages: the comprehensiveness of his view, its balance and sanity, its lack of petulance. Convinced of the general disastrousness of experience, he already knows that is not the whole story; he is resolved both to endure life and to enjoy it:

> Methinks we have hugely mistaken this matter of Life and Death. . . .Methinks my body is but the lees of my better being. In fact take my body who will, take it I say, it is not me. And therefore three cheers for Nantucket; and come a stove boat and stove body when they will, for stave my soul, Jove himself cannot.[1]

Ishmael's pervasive good humor bespeaks his wholeness—as Ahab's humorlessness bespeaks his deep sickness of spirit. Except in scorn, Ahab never smiles or laughs. But Ishmael is a splendidly risible being, full of "the spirit of godly gamesomeness" he so admires in the hilarious creature he names the Huzza Porpoise. His mirth differs, however, from the essentially reckless and frivolous jollity of a man like Stubb. It is Stubb who says, " 'Such a waggish leering as lurks in all your horribles!' " but it needs an Ishmael to see that the remark is profound. His is the responsible and intellectual humor of deep comedy, an enlightened irony, accepting positively the immense range of the absurd in human behavior and human destiny. It is a vision not really separable from the tragic vision, but spouse or partner within it.

An attractive humility, a wry self-knowledge, distinguishes Ishmael's vision of the tragic. Those qualities make his developing affection for Queequeg a gay as well as a touching affair. Thus, in trying to dissuade Queequeg from his over-scrupulous worship of Yojo, he "labored to show Queequeg that all these Lents, Ramadans, and prolonged ham-squattings in cold, cheerless rooms were stark nonsense; bad for the health; useless for the soul; opposed, in short, to the obvious laws of Hygiene and common sense." And we collect his humorous and ironic knowledge of the self and the race from a passing reflection: "...Heaven have mercy on us all—Presbyterians and Pagans alike—for we are all somehow dreadfully cracked about the head, and sadly need mending." The situation and the tone are comic, but we can push the thought as deep as we please.

Ishmael's wholeness, his possession of himself without need of defensive dignity, lets him move flexibly to form links with other men. Melville gives the trait rich expression in the chapter, "A Squeeze of the Hand," where Ishmael and others of the crew sit about a tub of sperm oil squeezing congealed lumps back into fluid. After a few minutes in the unctuous stuff, Ishmael says, "my fingers felt like eels, and began, as it were, to serpentine and spiralize." He feels himself partaking of a general lustration, a cleansing, particularly, of his obligation to the "horrible oath" of cooperation in Ahab's revenge.

> Squeeze! squeeze! squeeze! all the morning long; I squeezed that sperm till I myself almost melted into it; I squeezed that sperm till a strange sort of insanity came over me; and I found myself unwittingly squeezing my co-laborers' hands in it, mistaking their hands for the gentle globules. Such an abounding, affectionate, friendly, loving feeling did this avocation beget; that at last I was continually

squeezing their hands, and looking up into their eyes sentimentally; as much as to say,—Oh! my dear fellow beings, why should we longer cherish any social acerbities, or know the slightest ill-humor or envy! Come; let us squeeze hands all round; nay, let us squeeze ourselves into each other; let us squeeze ourselves universally into the very milk and sperm of kindness.

Would that I could keep squeezing that sperm for ever! For now, since by many prolonged, repeated experiences, I have perceived that in all cases man must lower or at least shift, his conceit of attainable felicity; not placing it anywhere in the intellect or the fancy; but in the wife, the heart, the bed, the table, the saddle, the fire-side, the country; now that I have perceived all this, I am ready to squeeze case eternally. In thoughts of the visions of the night, I saw long rows of angels in paradise, each with his hands in a jar of spermaceti.

The passage makes a grand lyrical affirmation of Hawthorne's "magnetic chain" of human relationship, the healthy capacity to supervene the locked-in self. To both writers, the solitary self is the sick self. This "inter-indebtedness" of men, which is ideal to Ishmael, to Ahab is insult. With a resonance from Macbeth. Ahab muses as he waits for the ship's carpenter to make him a new whale bone leg:

Here I am, proud as a Greek god, and yet standing debtor to this block head for a bone to stand on! Cursed be that mortal inter-indebtedness which will not do away with ledgers. I would be free as air; and I'm down in the whole world's books. I am so rich, I could have given bid for bid with the wealthiest Praetorians at the auction of the Roman empire (which was the world's); and yet I owe for the flesh in the tongue I brag with.[2]

When the Pequod leaves Nantucket on that short, cold Christmas and Bildad's hymn sounds through the wind and sleet, Ishmael, standing in his "wet feet and wetter jacket," cheerfully accepts the leading of the song to a vision of "many a pleasant haven in store," where are "meads and glades so eternally vernal, that the grass shot up by the spring, untrodden, unwilted,

remains at midsummer." But we come to see that his sanguine
spirit speaks out of a soundness of heart not easily won. It
meets cruel testing in the voyage, and survives and grows
because its roots are dense and complex. The ocean, as
emblematic of life, does indeed repeatedly offer him her smiling
aspect, meads and glades so seductively vernal that they seem
permanent and the whole of truth. Entranced by that ravishing
and mysterious beauty, Ishmael stands his mast-head in the guise
of a "sunken-eyed young Platonist"; but it is the power of his
own thought that recalls him to a harsher reality:

> . . .lulled into such an opium-like listlessness of vacant, unconscious
> reverie is this absent-minded youth by the blending cadence of waves
> with thoughts, that at last he loses his identity; takes the mystic ocean
> at his feet for the visible image of that deep, blue, bottomless soul,
> pervading mankind and nature; and every strange, half-seen, gliding,
> beautiful thing that eludes him; every dimly-discovered, uprising fin of
> some undiscernible form, seems to him the embodiment of those
> elusive thoughts that only people the soul by continually flitting
> through it. In this enchanted mood, thy spirit ebbs away to whence it
> came; becomes diffused through time and space; like Cranmer's
> sprinkled Pantheistic ashes, forming at last a part of every shore the
> round globe over.
>
> There is no life in thee, now, except that rocking life imparted
> by a gently rolling ship; by her, borrowed from the sea; by the sea,
> from the inscrutable tides of God. But while this sleep, this dream is
> on ye, move your foot or hand an inch; slip your hold at all; and
> your identity comes back in horror. Over Descartian vortices you
> hover. And perhaps, at mid-day, in the fairest weather, with one
> half-throttled shriek you drop through that transparent air into the
> summer sea, no more to rise for ever. Heed it well, ye Pantheists!

Ishmael's affirmativeness grows in fact from his habitual fullness
of view, a relativism that demonstrates his basic sanity, and
stands opposite to Ahab's obsessed absolutism. He tells us early
that he is "quick to perceive a horror"; but that understates the
depth and density of his tragic knowledge. The best sign of this

inclusiveness comes in the chapter of "The Try-Works." Watching from his post at the tiller, the hellish scene of the men tending the huge furnaces boiling down the oil, he feels that "the rushing Pequod, freighted with savages, and laden with fire, and burning a corpse, and plunging into that blackness of darkness, seemed the material counterpart of her monomaniac commander's soul." He is caught in a mesmeric trance, in which he turns himself about and is on the point of capsizing the vessel, when he comes to himself and rights the course. Recovering from his terrible shock, he chides himself for succumbing to the "artificial fire," and looks ahead to the clear and benign light of day, "the glorious, golden, glad sun, the only true lamp." But reflecting on the event he makes clear the immense ranges of sorrow over which his affirmation has asserted itself:

> Nevertheless the sun hides not Virginia's Dismal Swamp, nor Rome's accursed Campagna, nor wide Sahara, nor all the millions of miles of deserts and of griefs beneath the moon. The sun hides not the ocean, which is the dark side of this earth, and which is two-thirds of this earth. So, therefore, that mortal man who hath more of joy than sorrow in him, that mortal man cannot be true — not true, or undeveloped. With books the same. The truest of all men was the Man of Sorrows, and the truest of all books is Solomon's and Ecclesiastes is the fine hammered steel of woe. "All is vanity." ALL. This wilful world hath not got hold of unchristian Solomon's wisdom yet. But he who dodges hospitals and jails, and walks fast crossing graveyards, and would rather talk of operas than hell; calls Cowper, Young, Pascal, Rousseau, poor devils all of sick men; and throughout a care-free lifetime swears by Rabelais as passing wise and therefore jolly; — not that man is fitted to sit down on tomb-stones, and break the green damp mould with unfathomably wondrous Solomon.

But he is not through with the question yet, and in the closing paragraph of the chapter he again sets the sun and the fire side by side and shows the strenuous spiritual peace he has

made of their union. The metaphor is one of Melville's greatest
and most complex:

> Give not thyself up, then, to fire, lest it invert thee, deaden thee; as
> for the time it did me. There is a wisdom that is woe; but there is a
> woe that is madness.[3] And there is a Catskill eagle in some souls that
> can alike dive down into the blackest gorges, and soar out of them
> again and become invisible in the sunny spaces. And even if he for
> ever flies within the gorge, that gorge is in the mountains; so that even
> in his lowest swoop the mountain eagle is still higher than other birds
> upon the plain, even though they soar.

The image in fact is that of a *high* profundity; and to
understand that necessary paradox is to come close to the center
of Melville's thought in the novel. The eagle's triumph is really
over the abyss itself, the necessary abyss, that which must form
part of a total vision of life. That gorge is in the mountains in
that it is a due property of any high or profound speculation,
any fully mature facing of the facts of life. "There is a wisdom
that is woe; but there is a woe that is madness" can stand as a
text for the novel as a whole. The wisdom that is woe (or the
woe that is wisdom) can stand for Ishmael; the woe that is
madness is Ahab's absolutist hatred, his "inversion" by the fire.
Ahab cannot say, with Job, "Though he slay me, yet will I trust
in him"; it is Ishmael who refuses to refuse to love.

To express this sane rejection of nihilistic despair, Melville
draws other wonderful figures from the sea and the fishery.
Thinking of the marvel of the warm-blooded whale's ability to
live easily in Arctic waters, and speaking with the splendidly
serious wit for which we come to love him, Ishmael draws out
the analogy to man's need for a preservative integrity:

> . . .herein we see the rare virtue of a strong individual vitality, and the
> rare virtue of thick walls, and the rare virtue of interior spaciousness.
> Oh, man! admire and model thyself after the whale! Do thou, too,

remain warm among ice. Do thou, too, live in this world without being of it. Be cool at the equator; keep thy blood fluid at the Pole. Like the great dome of St. Peter's, and like the great whale, retain, O man! in all seasons a temperature of thine own.

Seeing the whale going about his business, his head surrounded by the vapor that Ishmael suggests is the element of the creature's "incommunicable contemplations," and which on occasion is "glorified" by a rainbow, he proceeds to a specifically theological formula, a sort of illuminated agnosticism:

For, d'ye see, rainbows do not visit the clear air; they only irradiate vapor. And so, through all the thick mists of the dim doubts in my mind, divine intuitions now and then shoot, enkindling my fog with a heavenly ray. And for this I thank God; for all have doubts; many deny; but doubts or denials, few along with them, have intuitions. Doubts of all things earthly, and intuitions of some things heavenly; this combination makes neither believer nor infidel, but makes a man who regards them both with equal eye.

In the great chapter of "The Grand Armada," with the Pequod in the Straits of Sunda, Ishmael's boat crew is drawn by a whale into a strange "enchanted calm" at the center of a vast and violent concourse of whales where they are witness to a sort of generative cycle of the great creatures, love-making, pregnancy, new birth. Ishmael again makes the analogy to the intricate totality of the self:

And thus, though surrounded by circle upon circle of consternations and affrights, did these inscrutable creatures at the centre freely and fearlessly indulge in all peaceful concernments; yea, serenely revelled in dalliance and delight. But even so, amid the tornadoed Atlantic of my being, do I myself still for ever centrally disport in mute calm; and while ponderous planets of unwaning woe revolve round me, deep down and deep inland there I still bathe me in eternal mildness of joy.

In an earlier and almost equally beautiful metaphor, his counterpoised elements are the sea and the land themselves. He moves from reflection on the "universal cannibalism" of the sea and the "devilish brilliance and beauty of many of its most remorseless tribes," to the kind of "linked analogy" that is the habit of his mind and the language of his faith:

> Consider all this; and then turn to this green, gentle, and most docile earth; consider them both, the sea and the land; and do you not find a strange analogy to something in yourself? For as this appalling ocean surrounds the verdant land, so in the soul of man there lies one insular Tahiti, full of peace and joy, but encompassed by all the horrors of the half known life. God keep thee! Push not off from that isle, thou canst never return!

That figure returns the mind uneasily to the still earlier apostrophe to the indomitable Bulkington, whose apotheosis was to "leap up" from his "ocean-perishing." There the land was the "slavish shore" and the sea wild and free: ". . .all deep, earnest thinking is but the intrepid effort of the soul to keep the open independence of her sea. . . ." Ishmael has reversed the terms of his metaphor, but he has not tampered with his conviction. The valuable life is the committed life. If you want to pursue Leviathanic truths, you must push off from the slavish shore into the terrible element of the whale:

> No. Only in the heart of quickest perils; only when within the eddyings of his angry flukes; only on the profound unbounded sea, can the fully invested whale be truly and livingly found out.

Then of course "you run no small risk of being eternally stove and sunk by him." Really deep, earnest thinking will turn any soul into a tornadoed Atlantic. Then it will compose its insular Tahiti, where it can centrally disport in mute calm, out of the resources of its preservative sanity, its affirmative gaiety, its intuitions of things heavenly, its acrobatics in the mountain gorge, its equal eye. We recall again the sea-gudgeon who "retires into" the mouth of the whale "in great security, and there sleeps." Ishmael's voyage is not less strenuous than Ahab's, it is only less frantic.

V

What, then, of the whale? The novel offers four basic readings. First, the whale is a commodity, peculiarly valuable. It is an accident of his nature and his element that he is peculiarly dangerous. He is a quarry and he must be hunted: it is the business of the Pequod and her crew to find him, kill him, dress him, and take him home. The members of the crew cooperate willingly with the exciting fiction that their quarry is Moby Dick alone; but fundamentally Starbuck speaks for their common commercial motive when he says, " '...I came here to hunt whales, not my commander's vengeance. How many barrels will thy vengeance yield thee even if thou gettest it, Captain Ahab? It will not fetch thee much in our Nantucket market.' " Secondly, the whale is "cetology," the Leviathan of the natural world, the most awful, the most amusing, and the most instructive of natural creatures. As such, Melville gives him thousands of words, none dull. As such, he is a huge piece of *scientia* to be anatomized and known as well as may be by a young man who wants to know about the real world of things. A robust, witty, and inventive sensibility like Ishmael's finds him, in his "linked analogies," an immense animate textbook in the nature of nature.

As a whale-hunt and as a textbook, *Moby Dick* is already a great book. But Melville is really driving four Leviathans, and it is the combination that makes of the novel something uniquely grand. With Ahab and with Ishmael we must "strike through the mask" to "the little lower layer"—to the two patterns of moral signification they find embodied in the whale. In reading the white whale, Ahab and Ishmael are reading the universe; they offer us counterpoised archetypes of man's response. The two visions are kin, as representatively human, even twinned, at times, as in the Siamese chapters, "Moby Dick" and "The Whiteness of the Whale." Ishmael feels the murderous attraction of Ahab's vision: "A wild, mystical, sympathetical feeling was in me; Ahab's quenchless feud seemed mine." Ahab feels that he has bent every will to his own mad "iron way": "...my one cogged circle fits into all their various wheels, and they revolve."[4] But Ishmael's will does finally separate and assert itself, and thenceforth the two visions move irreconcilably, a mad and a sane integrity. That the white whale means something not merely commercial, something ultimate and inclusive, is established early. Melville speaks in his first pages of the union of human speculation and the white whale's element: "...meditation and water are wedded for ever," and the waters of the world have offered us since time began "the image of the ungraspable phantom of life." In Moby Dick that image becomes "the gliding great demon of the seas of life." "And this is the key to it all," Melville says. The white whale incarnates mystery, *the* mystery, the enigma of meaning or design in the shape of the universe and the fate of man. Can man know him, and what does he say? Ahab and Ishmael present alternative readings of the mystery, and the dramatic action is shaped to render a judgment upon them both.

Ahab is convinced that the whale is significant, and that he has found the only right response to him. The relationship as he sees it is one of pure mutual hatred:

> He tasks me; he heaps me; I see in him outrageous strength, with an
> inscrutable malice sinewing it. That inscrutable thing is chiefly what I
> hate; and be the white whale agent, or be the white whale principal, I
> will wreak that hate upon him.

In passages of sustained hyperbolic grandeur, Melville sums up
Ahab's hysterical understanding of his destiny. Ahab's is the
grand kind of error that makes tragic story. He assumes first of
all that his fate has meaning; then that he can know that
meaning and that it is malign—that the universe has bothered to
hate him; finally that his wound is the sign of his election to
represent the race in the conflict with the gods. He is a huge
sayer of huge nays. It is all sublime egotism, and Ahab is a
Lucifer of men, godlike and ungodly, a deadly absolute.

   Ishmael's reading of the whale is less spectacular and more
complex. Time and circumstance do not press upon him as they
do upon Ahab: he is young, and the gods have not yet sent an
emblematical beast to bite off his leg. As a young man involved
in an education on the Yale-Harvard whale ship, he luxuriates in
learning. In his madly narrowed field of vision, Ahab can see
nothing but whales, and no whale but the white one. Ishmael's
horizon is wide and hospitable, and the whale is only the largest
visible object, the chief of many marvels. Ahab knows; Ishmael
is free to wonder, to doubt, to speculate and qualify. But
"Leviathan is the text," and it is chiefly in him, as fact and
symbol, that Ishmael luxuriates. As the whale sports in his own
native element, Ishmael sports, sensuously and intellectually, in
many moods, in a bath of words about the whale. His mind is
energetic, elastic, humorous, never solemn, beautifully serious.
The physiology of the whale fascinates him, and in his language
it fascinates us. So with the natural history of the whale. "Who
can show a pedigree like Leviathan?" he asks in a great passage:

Ahab's harpoon had shed older blood than the Pharaoh's. Methuselah seems a schoolboy, I look around to shake hands with Shem. I am horrorstruck at this antemosaic, unsourced existence of the unspeakable terrors of the whale, which, having been before all time, must needs exist after all humane ages are over.

But it is the mythology, or better, perhaps, the theology, of the whale, the white whale, that must concern us. Ishmael retails the myth of the white whale's "ubiquitousness," and that of his immortality, or "ubiquity in time," the awesome superstition that

> though groves of spears should be planted in his flanks, he would still swim away unharmed; or if indeed he should ever be made to spout thick blood, such a sight would be but a ghastly deception; for again in unensanguined billows hundreds of leagues away, his unsullied jet would once more be seen.

Ishmael does make, with Ahab, the great precipitating assumption that the universe is offered to man as a thing to know, and he has a duty to know it. The mystic ocean is the sea of significance, and the mystic whale is its focus and embodiment, the mystery at the heart of the mystery. Ishmael is appalled by the daring of the enterprise: "...to have one's hands among the unspeakable foundations, ribs, and very pelvis of the world; this is a fearful thing." He marvels at his own presumption (as Ahab never does): "....how may unlettered Ishmael hope to read the awful Chaldee of the sperm whale's brow?" And again, "What am I that I should essay to hook the nose of this Leviathan?" It is not required of man to hunt Leviathans; he can rest comfortable on the turnpike earth. But as Ishmael drily remarks, "...there is no *earthly* way of finding out precisely what the whales really looks like" [my italics]. If you want whales you must go to sea. And if you choose to pursue the whale, "You run no small risk of being eternally stove and sunk by him."

Ishmael has chosen to go to sea, ,and the sea chooses to offer him the whale of whales, the fact and the myth of Moby Dick. "It was the whiteness of the whale that above all things appalled me," he tells us; and he labors at length to explain that feeling—"else all these chapters might be naught." What "appals" him—Melville uses the word as a brutal pun—is the union of murderous power and benign aspect in one creature, his wearing of the color of "the innocence of brides, the benignity of age," and so on. He sums up the compound feeling of terror in beauty most economically in his footnote on the Polar bear, whose "heightened hideousness. . .only arises from the circumstance, that the irresponsible ferociousness of the creature stands invested in the fleece of celestial innocence and love. . . .were it not for the whiteness, you would not have that intensified terror." The paradox of whiteness, Ishmael feels, is not an illusion, not a poetical idea, but a true property of the natural world, a dreadful albino reality. Thinking of the albatross, for example, of "those clouds of spiritual wonderment and pale dread, in which that white phantom sails in all imaginations," Ishmael concludes, "Not Coleridge first threw that spell; but God's great, unflattering laureate, Nature."

What moves Ishmael's awe is the "instinct of the knowledge of the demonism of the world," the instinct of the buried "knowledge," that is, that "though in many of its aspects this visible world seems formed in love, the invisible spheres were formed in fright." So understood, the white whale is the messenger and the executioner from the invisible spheres where man is hated, where powers are busy designing his torture and annihilation. Yet Ishmael finds in the whiteness of the whale a still more terrible suggestion: "Is it that by its indefiniteness it shadows forth the heartless voids and immensities of the universe. . .?" Perhaps the Designer feels too little about us even to hate us—perhaps he feels nothing at all?

> Or is it, that as in essence whiteness is not so much a color as the visible absence of color, and at the same time the concrete of all colors; is it for these reasons that there is such a dumb blankness, full of meaning, in a wide landscape of snows — a colorless, all-color of atheism from which we shrink?

"A dumb blankness, full of meaning"—the meaning of which may be absolute meaninglessness.[5]

"Pondering all this," Ishmael says, all this dumbly speaking whiteness, "the palsied universe lies before us a leper." Reading it as the hatred of the gods, Ishmael is free to reel into Ahab's hysterical nihilism; reading it as cosmic indifference, he is free to reel into a wholly cynical rationalism. By doing neither, he saves his soul alive, and ultimately his body too. The great chapter from which I have been borrowing stands only a third of the way through the action, and its mood is in part a residue of Ahab's profane and hypnotic suasion exercised in the first of the terrific quarter-deck scenes, immediately preceding. In the action as a whole, Ishmael keeps his temper and he keeps his head: ultimately the case can be put as simply as that. What we see is a splendid speculative intelligence admitting that it cannot know the will of God, but resolving to keep itself sweet, finding no need to turn sour or frantic.

This does not mean that he decides that the universe is pretty after all; he finds it often deadly, often beautiful. He does not forget that life is an affair of tragedy, or that "the truest of all men was the Man of Sorrows." The white whale is not to be known. He embodies "the interlinked terrors and wonders of God." He is beautiful and terrible and he keeps his own counsel. Unlettered Ishmael cannot read the awful Chaldee of the sperm whale's brow. We are welcome to try to read it,

but Ishmael gives it up: "I but put that brow before you. Read
it if you can." Thinking of the blank ramparts of the whale's
featureless battering ram of a head, he says, "I say again he has
no face." There seems little doubt that Melville is making serious
play upon Jehovah's response to the plea of Moses that He
reveal Himself upon Mt. Sinai:

> Dissect him how I may, then, I but go skin deep; I know him not,
> and never will. But if I know not even the tail of this whale, how
> understand his head? much more, how comprehend his face, when
> face he has none? Thou shalt see my back parts, my tail, he seems to
> say, but my face shall not be seen. But I cannot completely make out
> his back parts; and hint what he will about his face, I say again he has
> no face.[6]

VI

Christian Starbuck takes the leap of faith: "I look deep
down and do believe." Manichaean Ahab says, in effect, "I will
kill what I can reach of the God who hates me." Agnostic
Ishmael says, in effect, "I hope and I fear, but I cannot know; I
am content." Restlessly but sanely he fights the good fight. To
compound his tropes and his geography, he is forever at sea now
in the tornadoed Atlantic of his spirit, but he carries his insular
Tahiti always inside him. In the irradiated vapor overhanging the
"vast, mild head" of the swimming whale, he has found the
linked analogy to his own mind. In the book's first reference to
the white whale, he is vaguely glimpsed as "one grand hooded
phantom, like a snow hill in the air." For Ishmael, at the end,
he is still hooded, and better so. In the storm-bound chapel of
the port, months back, before the voyage began, Father Mapple
had closed his sermon with the words, " 'I leave eternity to

Thee; for what is man that he should live out the life time of his God?' " For Ishmael the voyage is a long initiation, a slow accumulation of the wisdom necessary to that acceptance of human limits. The divine design is a mystery, baffling and terrible, but habitable with fortitude. Time gives to Ahab's madness an awful concentration; his fixed purpose consumes everything about him not itself; he is hot, dry, indurated with it, solid hate. But time brings size to Ishmael's sanity, and the form it takes is a warm and flexible brotherliness. With great good will, he lowers his "conceit of attainable felicity." He resolves to be merely and wholly human; he lives in what Alejo Carpentier has called The Kingdom of This World. The tub of sperm oil in which he grasps hands with his shipmates is a trope of the natural extreme unction of the accepted human state; it raises Hawthorne's theme to the pitch of poetry and myth.

This acceptance is not shallow or easy. What Ishmael accepts is the tension of dubiety, the necessary restlessness of the soul, the endlessness of the mystery of meaning. The best place to feel that complex affirmation is in that most moving of his soliloquies, the apostrophe with which he salutes a calm golden day at sea, shortly before the final catastrophe:

> Oh, grassy glades! oh, ever vernal endless landscapes in the soul; in ye, – though long parched by the dead drought of the earthly life, – in ye, men yet may roll, like young horses in new morning clover; and for some few fleeting moments, feel the cool dew of the life immortal on them. Would to God these blessed calms would last. But the mingled, mingling threads of life are woven by warp and woof: calms crossed by storms, a storm for every calm. There is no steady unretracing progress in this life; we do not advance through fixed gradations, and at the last one pause: – through infancy's unconscious spell, boyhood's thoughtless faith, adolescence' doubt (the common doom), then scepticism, then disbelief, resting at last in manhood's pondering repose of If. But once gone through, we trace the round again; and are infants, boys, and men, and Ifs eternally. Where lies the

final harbor, whence we unmoor no more? In what rapt ether sails the world, of which the weariest will never weary? Where is the foundling's father hidden? Our souls are like those orphans whose unwedded mothers die in bearing them: the secret of our paternity lies in their grave, and we must there to learn it.

There is no need to retell the story. "The weaver-god, he weaves...." Ahab chases with curses a Job's whales around the world, and one day, off the coast of Japan, they meet, and for the microcosm of the Pequod that is the end of the world. Before the end there is a final crazy Black Mass on the deck. Ahab stands holding the main-mast links in a violent storm as a "lofty tri-pointed trinity of flames" plays about the yard-arms, and speaks:

> 'Oh! thou clear spirit of clear fire, whom on these seas I as Persian once did worship, till in the sacramental act so burned by thee, that to this hour I bear the scar; I now know thee, thou clear spirit, and I now know that thy right worship is defiance. To neither love nor reverence wilt thou be kind; and e'en for hate thou canst but kill; and all are killed. No fearless fool now fronts thee. I own thy speechless, placeless power; but to the last gasp of my earthquake life will dispute its unconditional, unintegral mastery in me. In the midst of the personified impersonal, a personality stands here.

Ahab's "humanities" return, in a kind of lightening before death, in a beautiful scene with Starbuck just before the sighting of the white whale. As Ishmael reports the first full sight of Moby Dick, "A gentle joyousness — a mighty mildness of repose in swiftness, invested the gliding whale....not Jove, not that great majesty Supreme! did surpass the glorified White Whale as he so divinely swam." Thickly and blandly, the language deifies the creature; and out of sight under the water is that intangible malignity that has been from the beginning: "...the full terrors of his submerged trunk...the wrenched hideousness of his jaw." For the symbolical three days the chase continues, and the pagan mumbo-jumbo prophecy of Fedallah completes itself piece by piece.

At the end it is Ishmael who is "left alone to tell thee." "The unexplained survivor breaking off the nightmare," W. H. Auden puts it in his fine poem on Melville. But I have tried to show how Melville does explain, dramatically, why Ishmael may live. He saves himself, really, by deserving the complex symbolic mechanisms the action offers him at the end. He is sustained first by the life-buoy that has been cobbled out of Queequeg's coffin. The elongated Siamese ligature of that human love extends itself to Ishmael from the general ocean-perishing. And finally he is saved by the ship of the captain to whom inhuman Ahab had refused help in the search for the lost son: "It was the devious-cruising Rachel, that in her retracing search after her missing children, only found another orphan." Ishmael has asked, "Where is the foundling's father hidden?" He is himself an orphan human spirit. Nowhere in the book is there any mention of father or mother to him, of family of any kind.[7] He is himself, with himself to make, naked, whole, free-standing, a pure integrity. He is animula and ephebe, the seeking, self-defining soul. Not Ahab but Ishmael has earned the right to say, "a personality stands here." He has earned the right to survive by sustaining with a whole mind and heart initiation into an unqualified tragic truth. Ishmael is the moral hero of the tragic action. He is the embodiment and the spokesman of Melville's own superb courage and intelligence.

NOTES

[1] In passages that suggest an active animosity of God to man Melville tends to use pagan names for the deity.

[2] Compare *Macbeth*, III. iv. 21-25:

I had else been perfect,
Whole as the marble, founded as the rock,
As broad and general as the casing air;
But now I am cabin'd, cribb'd, confin'd, bound in
To saucy doubts and fears.

[3] Compare Keats, Letter to John Hamilton Reynolds, May 3, 1818: "Until we are sick, we understand not; – in fine, as Byron says [*Manfred*, I. i. 10: 'Sorrow is Knowledge.'], 'Knowledge is Sorrow'; and I go on to say that 'Sorrow is Wisdom' – and further for aught we can know for certainty 'Wisdom is folly'!"

[4] Compare *Hamlet*, III. iii. 15-22:

The cease of majesty
Dies not alone, but, like a gulf, doth draw
What's near it with it. It is a massy wheel,
Fixed on the summit of the highest mount,
To whose huge spokes ten thousand lesser things
Are mortis'd and adjoin'd; which, when it falls,
Each small annexment, petty consequence,
Attends the boisterous ruin.

[5] " 'Zeus is dead; his son Whirligig rules in his stead,' " muses Strepsiades in *The Clouds* of Aristophanes.

[6] Compare Exodus 33, 20-23:

And he said, Thou canst not see my face: for there shall no man see me, and live. And the Lord said, Behold, there is a place by me, and thou shalt stand upon a rock: And it shall come to pass, while my glory passeth by, that I will put thee in a cleft of the rock, and will cover thee with my hand while I pass by: And I will take away mine hand, and thou shalt see my back parts: but my face shall not be seen.

(See *Moby Dick or, The Whale*, ed. by Luther S. Mansfield and Howard P. Vincent [New York, 1952], p. 786.)

[7] There is a single passing reference to a step-mother.

Old Melville's Fable

V

Now that the careful work of Mr. Hayford and Mr. Sealts on the manuscript of *Billy Budd* has given us a text that we can read with confidence, it is time to think again about those questions which they notice in their commentary as having divided critics since the story was first published in 1924. Is the little novel a "testament of acceptance" or a "testament of resistance"? Is its central tendency "tragic" or "ironic"? And our ordinary critical questions are not yet certainly answered: what was Melville trying to say in this product of his last years; how is this old-man's story related, in kind and quality, to the masterwork of his early years, *Moby Dick*; what is it worth as a human document and a work of art? Unquestionably the new text reads with greater fluency, sharpness, and symmetry than the versions of Weaver and Freeman. No editor can get around the fact that Melville left the manuscript unfinished; what Mr. Hayford and Mr. Sealts have given us, we may guess, is the best possible penultimate text: as they cautiously phrase it, ". . .we give in the Reading Text the wording that in our judgment most closely approximates Melville's final intention had a new fair copy been made without his engaging in further expansion or revision." No evaluation of Billy Budd can be conclusive, for we can never know how Melville might have refined or shifted his emphases had he continued to revise. But the story *feels* finished now, and it is beautiful enough as it stands to deserve any amount of analysis and appreciation. The most useful approach lies in understanding the highly conscious and complex work of stylization in the story.

W. H. Auden's eloquent poem, "Herman Melville," still seems to me the noblest way into the story from outside:

> Towards the end he sailed into an extraordinary mildness,
> And anchored in his home and reached his wife
> And rode within the harbour of her hand,

And went across each morning to an office
As though his occupation were another island.

Goodness existed: that was the new knowledge
His terror had to blow itself quite out
To let him see it; but it was the gale had blown him
Past the Cape Horn of sensible success
Which cries: "This rock is Eden. Shipwreck here."

But deafened him with thunder and confused with lightning:
—The maniac hero hunting like a jewel
The rare ambiguous monster that had maimed his sex,
Hatred for hatred ending in a scream,
The unexplained survivor breaking off the nightmare—
All that was intricate and false; the truth was simple.

Evil is unspectacular and always human,
And shares our bed and eats at our own table,
And we are introduced to Goodness every day,
Even in drawing-rooms among a crowd of faults;
He has a name like Billy and is almost perfect
But wears a stammer like a decoration;
And every time they meet the same thing has to happen;
It is the Evil that is helpless like a lover
And has to pick a quarrel and succeeds,
And both are openly destroyed before our eyes.

For now he was awake and knew
No one is ever spared except in dreams;
But there was something else the nightmare had distorted—
Even the punishment was human and a form of love:
The howling storm had been his father's presence
And all the time he had been carried on his father's breast.

Who now had set him gently down and left him.
He stood upon the narrow balcony and listened:
And all the stars above him sang as in his childhood
"All, all is vanity," but it was not the same;
For now the words descended like the calm of mountains—
Nathaniel had been shy because his love was selfish—

But now he cried in exultation and surrender
"The Godhead is broken like bread. We are the pieces."

And sat down at his desk and wrote a story.

To Auden, it is clear, *Moby Dick* and *Billy Budd* are the poles of a lifetime's theological argument. The later story, presenting the homely, dramatic, and significant confrontation of human good and evil, is a corrective of *Moby Dick*, based on the "new knowledge" of the love of God, understood as ramified and terrible. Auden is one of those who read the story's motive as "acceptance": ". . .the words descended like the calm of mountains." But what is accepted is the tragic truth of the human condition in that configuration of ecstatic suffering which follows from the Father's will, the Son's atonement, and the imputation of Adam's guilt. And so the story's ecstatic cry, mingling "exultation and surrender," is a phrasing of the Christian mystery. All this seems to me essentially true. Of course the form of the story is not that of an ecstatic cry; it is the product of an ecstatic insight, not the ecstasy itself. Melville orders his ecstasy, by artifice stylized into art, in a form which we can humanly accept as realism and symbolism, at once art and life. The story contains one genuinely ecstatic moment, Billy's "God bless Captain Vere!" as he stands with the rope about his neck. Auden's poem knows all this, just as it knows "And sat down at his desk and wrote a story" is an ellipsis of the true fact of the composition. Mr. Hayford's and Mr. Sealt's analysis of the manuscript shows that Melville's process was a striking case of slow accretion and dramatization, extending over several years, in which meaning and feeling were gradually accumulated and refined.

The style of *Billy Budd* is a new one for Melville, new at least in degree; it is the codifying and perfection of tendencies latent in his writing from the beginning. It is a highly formal, highly literary manner, one that moves with a certain queerly impressive, courtly, arthritic grace. Almost any paragraph will serve to recall the flavor of that rhetoric:

> Such reiteration, along with the manner of it, incomprehensible to a novice, disturbed Billy almost as much as the mystery for which he had sought explanation. Something less unpleasingly oracular he tried to extract; but the old sea Chiron, thinking perhaps that for the nonce he had sufficiently instructed his young Achilles, pursed his lips, gathered all his wrinkles together, and would commit himself to nothing further.

It is an artifical and archaic mode, with a distinctly Old World air about it. That the style has comparatively little to do with the natural speech of men at the end of the nineteenth century when Melville was writing suggests the point of the matter. By detaching and elevating his language above ordinary discourse, Melville purposely distances and abstracts his narrative. The events of which he writes are already a century old, but his style is not so much eighteenth century as it is achronological, of no time: thus it is of all time. The effect helps to cast the event of 1797, already antique, loose in time, thereby in space, to distance them to the local anonymity of fable or legend—to push them toward myth.

Melville's narrative attitude had always been a problem in his style, never more troublesome than in the greatest of his works, *Moby Dick*. Who is his speaker, his narrative mask or persona; who tells the story? One could never be perfectly sure for long at a time. His tendency to hop into and out of focus is mastered for the first time in *Billy Budd*. Though the speaking voice is complex here, elusive and anonymous, we can sufficiently identify it and hold it still. Originally no doubt the voice is Melville's own; he occasionally bluntly employs the first person pronoun. But the "I" narrator does not insist upon himself; he quickly becomes someone less personal, more engaging, and more functional. What we soon begin to hear is the voice of a collective intelligence, a voice racial yet of special character, ruminative, at once practical and philosophic, experienced, knowledgeable, weary but not exhausted. The narrator is omniscient as relating to the events of which he speaks, but it is a diffident, uninsistent omniscience. He speaks with a certain detachment, stands at a certain willed distance from his people and their actions. There he allows himself considerable latitude of attention, varying degrees of intimacy and circumstantiality, and freedom to move about speculatively and analogically. Still keeping to his limits, he similarly modulates his tones of voice; he can be harsh or hortatory, reflective, ironic, wistful or even lyrical, but he never rants and never weeps. The indecisiveness of Melville's earlier narrative stances has become a liberty flexibly and systematically controlled. Auden was right about the "extraordinary mildness" and the "calm of mountains." Doubtless this grave, humorous, savoring, antique voice is Melville's all the way. But as an old man he has learned a new way to tell tragic story, and has put aside his confused romantic voices. The voice of *Billy Budd* is a classical voice, the sound of an ideal myth-maker.

I dwell upon the story as narrative and upon the narrative voice because these are important features of Melville's stylized method. He emphasizes narrative and curtails and subordinates drama, and the relative detachment of the narrative voice is a means to that end. Predominantly he recounts rather than presents his story, retails it, as it were, after the fact. The story contains a good deal of drama, and that excellent, but examination of any incident in full context shows that Melville has tended to reduce single episodes to a near minimum of circumstance. It is instructive to see how much invention of detail was needed in turning the story into a play and a motion picture—and how the tone and rhythm were altered in the process. The real drama of *Billy Budd* is not that of episodes, of parts, but the drama of the whole, that which accumulates in experiencing the total shape of its meaning and feeling. The outspun narrative, the tale rather than the drama, is the medium of fable and legend. It is to that end, the recounting of a sequence of events of profoundly homiletic significance, representative and fabular, that Melville is gracefully and powerfully driving.

The argument for *Billy Budd* as symbolic legend must be defended against apparently contrary statements in the text. Melville several times protests that he is involved in only a bit of homely truth-telling. The story, he says, "is no romance." He publicly refuses to invent any plausible chain of events to account for Claggart's "antipathy spontaneous and profound" to Billy—to justify it, that is, in the dramatic terms of "Radcliffian romance"; instead he will trust to the "realism" of the very "mysteriousness" of the phenomenon. He apologizes for the rough finish of the end of his tale by asserting the demands of simple candor.

> The symmetry of form attainable in pure fiction cannot so readily be achieved in a narration essentially having less to do with fable than with fact. Truth uncompromisingly told will always have its ragged edges; hence the conclusion of such a narration is apt to be less finished than an architectural finial.

We need not be bullied into taking any of this literally. One of the things accomplished by the light touch of Melville's narrative manner, the distance and abstraction of the speaker's grandsire tone, is our freedom to react flexibly to the tale; by not insisting, he gives us liberty to respond as we feel moved. One thing we must feel is that *Billy Budd* is more than a piece of "mere" history. Melville is clearly writing a fiction, and to that extent his disclaimers must be set aside in any case. Of course he is also writing a truth, in the sense that *Billy Budd* is a set of beautifully credible human events, in our cant term a bit of realism. The whole argument may be truistic or beside the point. Melville is practising a piece of fashionable and attractive literary double-talk. *Billy Budd* is both fact and fiction, both history and symbolic legend, and excellent in all kinds. That multiple richness is one thing that makes it a great story. And if as "truth uncompromisingly told" it has its ragged edges, as symbolic legend it is not "less finished than an architectural finial." Its nearly perfect symmetry of symbolic form is achieved through what I am calling stylization.

How does the stylization work in the story, and to what ends of meaning and feeling? The most obvious, the most troublesome, and the most useful of its means is an elaborate pattern of Christian, or scriptural, analogy. Is Melville writing a point-blank Christian allegory, with Vere as God, Claggart as Satan, Billy as Christ, or as Adam? Yes and no. One must keep hold of the fact that, whatever it is additionally, *Billy Budd* is first of all a perfectly viable, never incredible, realistic story. The much that it is in addition one hesitates to call allegory, because it moves too quickly, lightly, and unself-consciously, with none of the stiffness, plainness, and insistent dogmatic equivalence that we associate with the angular power of allegory. Melville is after something subtler, vaguer, more graceful, and ultimately more inclusive. He is not recreating scriptural story, but making analogical use of one myth to create another myth, using one "supreme fiction," in Wallace Stevens' phrase, to illustrate and enrich another.

Melville makes no direct specification of Billy in the guise of Christ. That association is suggested to us by his youth, his beauty, his purity, by aspects of his relationship to Vere and to Claggart, and of course by his "sacrifice." He is twice compared to Adam. The notion of Vere as God also comes less by specification than by atmosphere: his nickname, "Starry," and his patronymic stemming evidently from the root for "truth," his suggestive dignity and aloofness, his fatherly attitude to Billy, his local omnipotence, his function in the action as judge and executioner.

With Claggart the scriptural suggestions are more numerous and direct. Though "real" like everything else in the story, Claggart derives unmistakably from Milton's Satan, with some coloration from creatures of Hawthorne. All that we see and learn of him is reminiscent of the fallen angel metamorphosing into the serpent. If he is "the direct reverse of a saint," he must be some kind of devil. He is tall and spare, elegant in movement, with "silken jet curls," a general malign good looks marred by an unhealthy pallor and a protuberant chin. "He looked like a man of high quality," Melville says, and again we think of Lucifer. The "hint of something defective or abnormal in the constitution and blood" and his "depravity according to nature" suggest Lucifer's invention of sin, his self-generating evil. In the same way, the shipboard rumor of "some mysterious swindle whereof he had been arraigned at the King's Bench" recalls the expulsion from heaven. The Miltonic case goes on and on. If Billy is Adam before the fall, then Claggart is the "envious marplot of Eden," the "serpent" whose "reactionary bite" Billy has not yet felt. Claggart's envy, like Satan's in Eden, is ambivalently mixed with love, his expression sometimes showing "a touch of soft yearning, as if Claggart could even have loved Billy, but for fate and ban." And the whole satanic derivation is made anatomical again when "a red light would flash forth from his eye like a spark from an anvil in a dark smithy" (recalling also a half-dozen of Hawthorne's central confrontations); when, accusing Billy before Captain Vere, his "first mesmeric glance was one of serpent fascination; the last was as the paralyzing lurch of the torpedo fish"; and when, after tongue-tied Billy has struck his fatal blow, lifting Claggart's body is "like handling a dead snake."

But Melville pushes these Christian, or at any rate theological, analogies still farther, and one has to deal with them. "The angel must hang," Vere exclaims when Billy has struck Claggart dead at his feet. Just before, Billy has been described as "the transfixed one," standing "like one impaled and gagged," his expression is "like that of a condemned vestal priestess in the moment of being buried alive," and a moment later it is "as a crucifixion to behold." Billy's hanging is surely in one sense sacrificial, made necessary by the past and potential sins of others. Again we must recall the agony in the garden as we watch the quick and lovely, though limited, spiritualization of Billy (Melville calls it his "agony") which is handled in the narrative with such grace and delicacy. He lies "prone in irons" in his soiled white clothes in one of the bays of the gun deck which branch "like small confessionals or side-chapels in a cathedral," and his turn from youth toward manhood shows itself in a single touching sign, a certain sharpening of the bone in the cheek. There can be no mistaking the Christian reference of the hanging itself; cast in that gorgeous lyrical sentence, it combines the crucifixion and the ascension in a single mystical moment:

> At the same moment it chanced that the vapory fleece hanging low in the East was shot through with a soft glory as of the fleece of the Lamb of God seen in mystical vision, and simultaneously therewith, watched by the wedged mass of upturned faces, Billy ascended; and

ascending, took the full rose of the dawn.

There follows the miraculous ("phenomenal") absence of muscular spasm in the hanged body. For years, we are told, the sailors kept track of the spar, for to them "a chip of it was as a piece of the Cross."

Clearly all these references do exist, and it is useless to pretend that they have no meaning. But any attempt to simplify the pattern into a plain holy-unholy triangle, a straightforward allegory of one-for-one significations, runs aground on practical and psychological objections. It is easier to believe that men are devils than that they are gods. Whereas the mind can contain the idea of Claggart as an embodiment of Satan, it is quickly embarrassed by other, more sacred, associations. Melville has realized all this, and intended it, and has provided the means in the text for limiting and qualifying the allegory, restraining it to be no more than hauntingly suggestive. He equips Billy and Vere to remind us of gods, but he is careful to root their feet in clay. Billy's innocence is not the product of divine insight; though it is always beautiful, its sources lie in inexperience and in something it is hard not to call stupidity. He is not flawless but flawed, and in a way that is profoundly human; his poverty of speech, culminating in his stammering muteness, is of the mind as well as the body, and must be set against the divine arti- culateness. And whatever the extenuations, he does come to the sacrifice with blood on his own hands. Similarly, Vere's limited field of vision, the relative narrowness and shortness of his moral range, the stubborn stolidity with which he accepts the bonds of institutions merely and coarsely human, are the properties of a man and not a god—though complex enough to need our examination and forgiveness. If we try to carry the holy allegory all the way, we bump finally against the absurdity of translating Billy's last words "God bless Captain Vere!" as "God bless God!" (though we may still hear even within that chagrin the distant echo of "Not my will but thine be done").

Melville commits these inconsistencies not because he did not know how to construct an allegory but because he had other meanings in mind. He is not trifling with us, and he does not put together an elaborate frame of Christian reference for any frivolous purpose. It is not merely decorative, it is structural. But we must complicate the matter further, as Melville does, to get at his purpose. In addition to his apparent New Testament tropes, he surrounds his persons with other ranges of analogy drawn from other portions of scripture and from pagan and secular sources. It is the total configuration that makes the meaning, rounds the inclusiveness of the homiletic design. Melville moves by means of a basic realistic tale, ornamented, enriched, and exemplified by history, legend, literature, Christian and pagan myth—the whole available store of human typology.

Billy is established from the beginning as a representative of a secular type, the type of the "Handsome Sailor," who combines "strength and beauty," "comeliness and power," and who is given a kind of secular worship by the other sailors because he is the perfection of themselves. He is "Aldebaran among the lesser lights of his constellation"; or he is looked at by his fellows with "that sort of pride. . .which the Assyrian priests doubtless showed for their grand sculptured Bull." Actually he is referred to more often in pagan terms than in directly Christian ones—compared to Apollo, Hercules, Achilles, Alexander. But the analogies are always woven into the tissue of actions directly present. Vere and Claggart are rooted with even greater firmness in the real world. It is no trouble at all to believe in them as real men on real human errands. All three men are fixed in the year 1797, in the naval wars of that year, and in the uneasy psychology that "lurkingly survived" a dangerous real event, the English naval mutinies at Spithead and the Nore. The whole tale is set in a full and convincing historicity. But then Melville draws analogues from the deeds of Nelson and from the fatal events on the American brig *Somers*, both of which have for him much of the quality of legend. He calls ships by such names as *Rights of Man* and *Bellipotent* and *Athée*. He installs a wizard in the narrative, an "old Merlin" called the Dansker. He makes his narrative persona summon other shadowy personae who are really forms of the author himself: "a writer whom few know," and "an honest scholar, my senior." He thickens and thickens the scriptural references, including many from the Old Testament, David and Saul, the sale of Joseph's coat, Abraham and Isaac, the judgment of Ananias. He finishes off his tale with an "official" account of his events in a naval chronicle, grotesquely false in detail and in spirit, and with a factitious sailor ballad, rude and ordinary and unspecific. We have to keep it all together to see what he is driving at, and by what means. This is complex artifice indeed. The story is made of a mingling of methods, a sweet and fluent fusion of many small artifices, repeated and woven, to form the grand artifice which is myth, the representative symbolic legend of the human condition on earth.

To see all this at work we need to return to the image of Billy as Adam, which must ultimately displace the image of Billy as Christ. There can be no doubt that the central dramatic and philosophic line of *Billy Budd*, the activating analogue, is born in the great myth of *Paradise Lost*. *Billy Budd* is a type of the archetype of the Fall of man, "with loss of Eden," the great rectangular pattern of Pride, Fall, Punishment, Rebirth which forms the rhythm of man's fate, the Ur-myth which underlies all tragic story in the Christian world. Melville twice directly compares Billy to Adam: he is "little more than a sort of upright barbarian, much such perhaps as Adam presumably might have been ere the urbane Serpent wriggled himself into his company"; and he is "a fine specimen of the *genus homo*, who in the nude might have posed for a statue of young Adam before the Fall." He makes other references in which only the name is lacking: for example, Billy is "a sound human creature, one to whom not yet has been proffered the questionable apple of knowledge"; and his nature is one that "in its simplicity never willed malice or experienced the reactionary bite of that serpent." We need to notice the light touch, the un-insistence, the suggestive dubiety that follows from the stylized conditional forms of Melville's rhetoric: Billy "might have posed," he is "little more than a sort of," "much such perhaps," "as Adam presumably might have been." I think the point of the chatty wordiness is not to insist that Billy "is" Adam, but that they mutually resemble: Adam is as much like Billy as Billy is like Adam. The great thing that they have in common is innocence; they are mutual types of untried, well-wishing purity which has to be tried in a world conceived as typical and which, as the Dansker drily reflects, is "not without some mantraps." *Billy Budd* then is a parable of man in the trap that is the world.

In the story the only thing more beautiful than Billy's innocence is the beauty of what happens to it. Melville spends more space in creating that innocence than on any other theme, and under his loving and graceful treatment it turns into something infinitely touching. One can feel the aged and disappointed author, "a writer whom few know," molding his snow image, working with a catch in the throat to form his pure youth at the threshold of the impure world. Though it would be a pleasure to rehearse the texts, there is not time to do so, and perhaps no need, for their function is the important question. For clear reasons, Melville makes Billy exactly twenty-one, at the point of his majority. His beauty, though it is scarcely intellectual at all, is as much spiritual as it is physical. It is also nearly as much feminine as it is masculine. Though Melville carefully emphasizes Billy's brawny healthfulness, a strain of fineness and unstudied delicacy turns it not effeminate so much as androgynous or angelic. This almost sexless and unconscious anonymity is the point of his purity. For Billy represents the "potential" beauty of man, the extreme of the mortally possible. I say mortally because Melville has made the world of his story unquestionably postlapsarian. Billy's stutter, which Melville calls a signature of "the envious marplot of Eden," tells us that he is a fallible man in the fallen world. But in every instinct he is the best the race can offer. In making Billy an orphan, "a foundling, a presumed by-blow," Melville returns with similar purpose to a motif of forty years earlier, the orphan Ishmael of *Moby Dick*; he had always loved the "isolatoes" of the race. "I have heard," says Billy cheerfully, "that I was found in a pretty silk-lined basket hanging one morning from the knocker of a good man's door in Bristol." His whole appearance indicates "a lineage in direct contradiction to his lot." "Noble descent was as obvious in him as in a blood horse." When an officer asks him, "Who was your father?" Billy answers, "God knows, sir." In other words, Billy, though he is not Christ, is a true son of God. His is the essential racial aristocracy: like Adam, he is made in God's image.

Melville carries his biblical and Miltonic imagery of the Fall an interesting further step. He speaks of Billy's kind of natural purity, his possession of "certain virtues pristine and unadulterate," as of the order of qualities "exceptionally

transmitted from a period prior to Cain's city and citified man."
This is to make of Billy a creature of primitive innocence who
has to make his own way in a "civilized" world, a fully ramified
postlapsarianism. Melville's trope for that world is the city (his
serpent is "urbane"), and he goes on to instance Caspar Hauser,
"wandering dazed" in a "Christian capital," and to quote
Martial's lines,

> Honest and poor, faithful in word and thought,
> What hath thee, Fabian, to the city brought?

Billy's purity of mind, heart, and body Melville frankly labels
"primitive," and one comes to see that "primitive" is one of the
quietly obsessive words of the text, a lightly emphatic leitmotif.
The word, or ideas rising out of the word, associate themselves also with Vere and Claggart and thus with the whole moral triangle
they compose with Billy. The air of aristocracy, for example, is
common to the three, and is not unrelated to the idea of the
primitive in Melville's sense. We have noted Billy's "noble
descent." Claggart, we are told, "looked like a man of high
quality"; "his brow was of the sort phrenologically associated
with more than average intellect"; and his "aspect and manner
were. . .suggestive of an education and career incongruous with
his naval function"; shipboard rumor reputes him "a *chevalier*"
incognito. Vere is unmistakably a gentleman. His ascendancy on
his ship is as much social and intellectual as it is official. Melville
makes him "allied to the higher nobility" and gives him a
bearing which in every way "suggests a virtue aristocratic in
kind." I think he means us to understand each of these figures
as the best of its kind, the perfection of a form. They are types
but they are high types, high stylizations of central facts of
man's nature and fate which they can show forth best because
they are pure forms. They are not far removed from Platonic

Ideas. The "aristocracy" is related to the "primitive" in this sense of genetic purity.

But Claggart and Vere are primitive in plainer and more significant ways. Claggart is incarnated Evil. He embodies the mysterious and immedicable presence of that primitive essence in the world. He is a "peculiar human creature the direct reverse of a saint." We will never understand him, Melville warns, if our notions of human wickedness are "limited to ideas of vulgar rascality." On board the ship, only "the old sea Chiron" the Dansker, with his "eccentric unsentimental old sapience, primitive in its kind," sees nearly to the center of Claggart's foul heart. Melville makes his point about Claggart's wickedness partly by the elaborateness of his refusal to account for it rationally. Its irrationality and unaccountableness are precisely what make it primitive and archetypal. To Claggart's "antipathy spontaneous and profound" toward the goodness incarnate in Billy, Melville applies the word "mystery," another of the obsessive words of the text. Claggart's is "the mania of an evil nature, not engendered by vicious training or corrupting books or licentious living, but born with him and innate. . . ." To "define" Claggart's "mystery of iniquity" he borrows a phrase and a gnomic gloss from Plato: "Natural depravity: a depravity according to nature." We might come a bit closer to understanding such a moral phenomenon as Claggart, Melville says drily through his narrative mask, "if that lexicon which is based on Holy Writ were any longer popular."

Captain Vere is by far the most complex figure in the story, in nature and in function. By any ordinary mortal standard he is an admirable man—a skilled seaman, an intrepid warrior, a just and powerful commander, an inflexibly upright and honorable human being. A stiffness in his personal presence is softened by "a certain unaffected modesty of manhood." In extreme contrast to Billy Budd, he is a lover of books, "with a marked leaning toward everything intellectual." His reading takes a practical cast; he loves books "treating of actual men and events. . .history, biography, and unconventional writers like Montaigne, who, free from cant, and convention, honestly and in the spirit of common sense philosophize upon realities." There is "a queer streak of the pedantic running through him": in a discussion he is apt to support a point by reference to ancient history. His social and political bias is conservative, but "disinterestedly" so, resting on carefully considered convictions and wishing well to man. He is not wholly unimaginative or unspeculative: on occasion he will stand with one hand in the rigging and "absently gaze off at the blank sea" with "a certain dreaminess of mood." But basically his is a stored and resolute pragmatic intelligence. Melville finds some irony in the appellation of "Starry Vere" to "one who whatever his sterling qualities was without any brilliant ones." The name is perfectly appropriate, however, to the loftiness and purity of his moral nature.

In fact Vere is as good a man as one could hope to find. Again that is the point of his character: that it is both excellent and inadequate. His character is "primitive" in the sense that it embodies something like the perfection of ordinary human nature, the limited creature. His heart is pure, his nerve is true, his mind is clear and vigorous in its working. But he is powerless to prevent, or significantly to ameliorate, a tragedy of injustice. That fact stands at the center of the fable: the best mind available is not good enough, the purest human will is powerless to deal with the ironic shape of experience. The analysis of the manuscript by Hayford and Sealts shows that Melville conceived his characters one by one in the slow and ruminative process of composition, first Billy, then Claggart, then Vere. Thus he posits innocence, its opposite, and a mediating judge, the symmetrical components of a standard moral emergency. In Billy, primitive pre-intellectual innocence is set moving in the mantrap world. It is attacked by an instinctive and non-rational malignity which hates innocence for being and for being beautiful. Stricken mute and aghast, innocence lashes out and unwillingly destroys its adversary. Intelligence adjudicates the case and can do no better than retributively to destroy the good.

Melville seems to me to be only marginally interested in the question of Captain Vere's "guilt." He deals with it only enough to preserve the running realism of his tale. What is much more central to his purpose is Vere's helplessness, his human incapacity to save the good alive. The sequence of his three exclamations at the scene of Claggart's killing needs to be recalled. "Fated boy!" he says "in almost a whisper" as Claggart falls; when the surgeon has confirmed the death, Vere cries, "It is the divine judgement of Ananias"; and after a moment's thought, "Struck dead by an angel of God! Yet the angel must hang." At once he is wholly aware of both the reality and the symbolism of the event, wholly clear on the distribution of guilt, and already wholly committed to his own limitation, what Ahab would have called "the iron way" within which he will be constrained to act. I think Melville is saying that there is no right way for Vere to act; he does the best he can, and the best can do no more than preserve order. Melville means the case to be representative. As Billy is not Christ, Vere is not God, and yet he is required to play God, the creature to mime the creator. Of course he must fail. It is "the way things are," an habitual pattern of experience. Vere is handed a flawed mechanism of excessive delicacy, an "enigma," a "mystery of iniquity," and commanded to repair it with his strong but hopelessly clumsy tools, his good heart, his common sense, his rationalistic penetration, his fidelity to social obligation.

Vere does not act wrongly, he acts necessarily. He is the prisoner of his own honorable convictions and of a constraining fate. Committed by conviction to the conservative virtue of order, "forms, measured forms," and to a military duty he understands as sacred, and by fate to the extraordinary situation of threatened mutiny, he does not what is right but what, as he must see it, is less wrong. He is perfectly clear on the issues: "Not, gentlemen, that I hide from myself that the case is an exceptional one. Speculatively regarded, it well might be referred to a jury of casuists"; and he is fully aware of the awfulness of the choice, or the lack of choice. He does not flinch from phrasing the full fatal ironies before Billy and the officers of the drumhead court. He has to move against the deepest leadings of his heart, against mercy and love. Melville shows him pacing his cabin, "climbing the slant deck in the ship's lee roll, without knowing it symbolizing thus in his action a mind resolute to surmount difficulties even if against primitive instincts strong as the wind and the sea." The conflict, as he bluntly expresses it, lies between Nature and law, and law must win:

'How can we judge to summary and shameful death a fellow creature innocent before God, and whom we feel to be so? — Does that state it aright? You sign sad assent. Well, I too feel that, the full force of that. It is Nature. But do these buttons that we wear attest that our allegiance is to Nature? No, to the King.'

For them, "acting not as casuists or moralists," it must be "a case practical," and Billy must die. "At the Last Assizes it shall acquit," Vere says of the plea of Billy's essential innocence. But these present assizes are only human, martial, and penultimate: Vere cannot be the Great Judge, he is only a local Justice of the Peace. He signs sad assent.

I see no doubt in the text that Melville forgives Vere for all this, finds it orderly and appropriate if heartbreaking, ironically shapely, and pities Vere not less than he pities Billy. The experience shakes Vere to the bottom of his being. Like Billy, Vere undergoes his agony; Melville calls it "the agony of the strong." But he never doubts that he has done what he had to do, the best "right" open to him. When he lies dying of his wound from the *Athée*, he murmurs the name of "Billy Budd, Billy Budd"; but these were "not the accents of remorse." Melville blames nobody in the story, not even Claggart: If you carry about an innate depravity, that is what you work with. His only definite denunciation -is of war itself, the outright criminality of it. Billy is doubtless "a martyr to martial discipline." Melville points his attack through the ship's chaplain, who, though he is too good a Christian to press his doctrinal case, seeing that "innocence was even a better thing than religion wherewith to go to Judgment," is nonetheless ironically "the minister of the Prince of Peace serving in the host of the God of War"; he is "as incongruous as a musket would be on the altar at Christmas" because "he lends the sanction of the religion of the meek to that which practically is the abrogation of everything but brute Force."

Melville's lifelong passionate hatred of war, coming to brief and bitter point, makes *Billy Budd* a powerful pacifist document— among other things. War is only a part of the pattern, its crudities and cruelties only a type of the general inextricable dilemma of human destiny. Who is to blame, Melville seems to say, if not the Designer, call him God or Fate? Melville uses that old word with an old-fashioned candor and precision that restores it to a Greekish purity. Billy is "Fated boy!" He lies between two great guns on the deck in the night before his execution, "as nipped in the vise of fate." Claggart "could even have loved Billy but for fate and ban." Melville bluntly specifies Claggart's uncontrollable devilishness and the Designer's responsibility:

> With no power to annul the elemental evil in him though readily
> enough he could hide it; apprehending the good, but powerless to be
> it; a nature like Claggart's, surcharged with energy as such natures
> almost invariably are, what recourse is left to it but to recoil upon
> itself and, like the scorpion for which the Creator alone is responsible,
> act out to the end the part allotted it.

He presents Billy, Claggart and Vere all "as nipped in the vise of
fate," and their story as the tragic fable of standard human
experience.

To reassemble our feeling about the story, perhaps the best
way is to read again the longish paragraph which is Melville's
treatment of the last interview, after the sentence of death,
between Billy and Vere, "each radically sharing in the rarer
qualities of our nature." The narrative voice speaks here in a
hushed whisper, as if of a thing too private and holy to be
directly overlooked, tells it as a myth and a mystery, probable
but inscrutable:

> It would have been in consonance with the spirit of Captain Vere
> should he on this occasion have concealed nothing from the
> condemned one—should he indeed have frankly disclosed to him the
> part he himself had played in bringing about the decision, at the same
> time revealing his actuating motives. On Billy's side it is not
> improbable that such a confession would have been received in much
> the same spirit that prompted it. Not without a sort of joy, indeed, he
> might have appreciated the brave opinion of him implied in the
> captain's making such a confidant of him. Nor, as to the sentence
> itself, could he have been insensible that it was imparted to him as to
> one not afraid to die. Even more may have been. Captain Vere may
> have in end developed the passion sometimes latent under an exterior
> stoical or indifferent. He was old enough to have been Billy's father.
> The austere devotee of military duty, letting himself melt into what
> remains primeval in our formalized humanity, may in end have caught
> Billy to his heart, even as Abraham may have caught young Isaac on
> the brink of resolutely offering him up in obedience to the exacting

behest. But there is no telling the sacrament, seldom if in any case revealed to the gadding world, whenever under circumstances at all akin to those here attempted to be set forth two of great Nature's nobler order embrace. There is privacy at the time, inviolable in the survivor; and holy oblivion, the sequel to each diviner magnanimity, providentially covers all at last.

The passage is deeply and honestly moving, and it says all the necessary things for itself. One need notice directly only the grace and gravity of the narrative tone, and the way the idea of the sanctity of the meeting is built into the texture of the diction, made organic with it, not decoratively overlaid. For whether Melville's context is Christian or not, it is surely theological. We are being asked to think of the fate of man, and the fable of Abraham and Isaac exemplifies the fable of Billy and Captain Vere; and vice versa; they are mutually illustrative. But they are not interchangeable; for we are in the real world now, and whereas the Voice commands Vere as Abraham, nobody comes forward at last to proffer the sacrificial lamb in place of the beloved son.

The issue as to whether the story is tragedy or irony seems to me quite clear. Of course the story is "tragic" and "a tragedy"; its content and its means are brutally ironic, tragic irony. In *Moby Dick* Melville recalled that his persons were "an old whale hunter" and "meanest mariners, and renegades and castaways," and commented on his own boldness in daring to "weave round them tragic graces." A passage to similar effect occurs in *Billy Budd*:

Passion, and passion in its profoundest, is not a thing demanding a palatial stage whereon to play its part. Down among the groundlings, among the beggars and rakers of the garbage, profound passion is enacted. And the circumstances that provoke it, however trivial or mean, are no measure of its power. In the present instance that stage is a scrubbed gun deck, and one of the external provocations a man-of-war's man's spilled soup.

Melville speaks of his events as "tragedy" no fewer than seven times. Primarily he is using the term in the old-fashioned folk sense, as describing the disastrous and more or less unaccountable things that happen to ordinary people. That such are his materials does not seem to me to disqualify the story as fully tragic. *Billy Budd* lacks nothing of formal literary tragedy, as classically defined, except the Aristotelian loftiness of persons and the Aristotelian dramatic form. Spiritually, where it matters most, the story is true tragedy. It is a lofty branch of the grand central myth that informs all tragic myth. By the dignity of his humble persons and the stateliness of his narrative mode, forming not a drama but a legend, Melville makes literary tragedy out of folk tragedy. His meanest mariners act out the mysterious and beautiful fatality of the race of man and his life in time. His narrative form is a very pure form, looser and more luxuriant than the dramatic, but elegantly controlled, grave, quiet, perfectly proportioned, reticently but precisely spoken. It is a form worthy of the most serious subject, and it is that to which the form is applied.

Nor can we properly find raggedness and inconsequence in the seemingly odd little movements that follow the hanging in the story. We can never know what changes Melville might have made if he had lived, but the sequence as it stands has for me the feeling of a right intentional shape. The effect of these little chapters, of the death of Vere, the garbled and unfair account of events in a "naval chronicle," the rudely lovely, anonymous and unspecific sailor ballad of "Billy in the Darbies," is at once to broaden and thicken the collective ironies and to extend the tight little representative tale onward in time and outward in space and in the common consciousness—to move it more and more toward legend. The position of the ballad at the end of all makes a rough diagram of Pater's thought that all art "aspires to the condition of music"; indeed, what is the whole story but a gravely graceful, extended lyric? A certain acidifying effect comes through in these last chapters, too, something like a bit of subtly ironic comedy, that insists again that we have been in the presence not of pathos but of tragedy. Melville's persons, like Yeats's right tragic actors, "do not break up their lines to weep." So behaving, they speak for Melville. The control of their voices is Melville's self-control, and *Billy Budd* is his classical response to *Moby Dick's* romantic cry. The eternal homesickness of Melville's soul is not less present. If *Billy Budd* is a testament of acceptance, the acceptance lies not at all in the logic but in the art, its modest and efficient formalization. The logic of the story does not accept the rightness of tragic destiny as exemplified by Billy's innocence, Claggart's wickedness, and Vere's helplessness. But the art accepts and celebrates the symmetry of its necessity, the comeliness of its terrible mystery.

The House of Yeats

VI

It is now perfectly clear that William Butler Yeats is a classic, a man for all seasons, one of the great poets. T. S. Eliot described him generously but not extravagantly when he called him "the greatest poet of our time—certainly the greatest in this language, and so far as I am able to judge, in any language." Yeats may also have been a great man, though that is a harder judgment to make, and is perhaps not our business.

I wish to praise the poet under the title of "The House of Yeats." Under that roof, or umbrella, I am thinking of the house as the family, in the Greek sense, 'the house of Atreus,' for example, which bore the famous curse; also of Yeats's own deep familial or dynastic sense of himself and his origins; also of his feudal, courtly, aristocratic leanings, which need to be defined and qualified; finally of actual houses which in the course of his life accommodated him with an air of purpose and symbolism. I find my most inclusive text in a remark of Frank O'Connor's: ". . .he was the most consistently noble man I have ever met." It is the nobility of Yeats, in its ramified and often surprising forms, that I wish to try to identify.

Confident as he was of his own creative gifts, Yeats never supposed that he had made himself; to be "self-born" (in his own phrase) was the privilege of gods or demons. Yeats was a Yeats, which is to say a union of Yeats and Pollexfen. It was his father who spoke what the poet called "the only eulogy that ever turned my head," as follows: " 'by marriage with a Pollexfen we have given a tongue to the sea cliffs.' " There is a great deal of Yeats in that statement, and in his pride in it. By "we" the father means we Yeatses and I John Butler Yeats. The tongue is the poet-son whom he loved and admired (and instructed). The sea cliffs are the tough tongue-tied Cornish Pollexfens. What most moves the son in the eulogy is to be declared the voice of the noble vision, of the world seen as high, deep, and hard, an arena of tragic experience: to be that sternness softened to the point of speech.

In seeking to understand the meaning of nobility in the life and work of Yeats, I shall glance quickly at a good many passages in his poetry and prose, and longer at four major poems: first that which Eliot called "the violent and terrible epistle dedicatory" to his volume of 1914, *Responsibilities*; then the title poem from *The Tower* of 1928; then two of the great *Last Poems* of 1939, "The Municipal Gallery Revisited" and "High Talk."

First the "Introductory Rhymes" of 1914:

> Pardon, old fathers, if you still remain
> Somewhere in ear-shot for the story's end,
> Old Dublin merchant 'free of ten and four'
> Or trading out of Galway into Spain;
> Old country scholar, Robert Emmet's friend,
> A hundred-year-old memory to the poor;
> Merchant and scholar who have left me blood
> That has not passed through any huckster's loin,
> Soldiers that gave, whatever die was cast:
> A Butler or an Armstrong that withstood
> Beside the brackish waters of the Boyne
> James and his Irish when the Dutchman crossed;
> Old merchant skipper that leaped overboard
> After a ragged hat in Biscay Bay.
> You most of all, silent and fierce old man,
> Because the daily spectacle that stirred
> My fancy, and set my boyish lips to say,
> 'Only the wasteful virtues earn the sun';
> Pardon that for a barren passion's sake,
> Although I have come close on forty-nine,
> I have no child, I have nothing but a book,
> Nothing but that to prove your blood and mine.

How much Yeats is there. Periodically, throughout his life, Yeats felt compelled to write what I think of as roll-calling poems,

poems of accountancy and summation, in which persons and motives were commanded to stand forth and shape up, to express and to embody the current, and collective, state of his mind and heart. This is such a poem. W. H. Auden has praised Yeats as the poet who brought back to life in English the occasional poem, verses that celebrate notable events. Auden was thinking of poems like "Easter 1916" or "In Memory of Major Robert Gregory," which are also roll-calling poems in my sense.

But these "Introductory Rhymes" are not quite the kind of thing Auden had in mind. Here the only occasion is personal and small, the publication of a new volume of poems and the poet's arrival at a certain age. Yet Yeats characteristically chooses to make ceremony of these small events. As he writes the poem in January 1914, he is forty-eight years old; but he does not say "forty-eight," he says "close on forty-nine." What he is thinking of is "fifty," the half-century, a small-scale *magnus annus*. For a man of Yeats's passionate and committed humanism, every event, because it is life and is human, is potentially symbolic and entitled to celebration. His sense of life was like Keats's, who spoke of "a life like the Scriptures, figurative," and guessed that Shakespeare "led a life of allegory" upon which his works were a "commentary." That sort of view of experience as allegory, rising out of myth and pointing back to it, was Yeats's view of his own life, indeed of all life.

Here, calling the roll at close on forty-nine, casting up a balance, Yeats is looking at his life as figurative, a metaphor full of meaning. It scarcely matters, or matters positively, that the event he is celebrating is negative, a non-event; the thing that is occurring is a non-occurrence. What he is celebrating is his own failure to create and transmit life: "I have no child, I have nothing but a book." The poem is a public and passionate *apologia pro vita sua*, asking pardon of the ranked shades of his ancestors,

"Pardon, old fathers," for his failure as a man and as a Yeats. At the same time the poem is a form of prayer. Characteristically, the gods who are supplicated are secular and familial: "Pardon, old fathers." As a child, Yeats tells us in his *Autobiography*, he had confused one of these household gods, the "silent and fierce old man," his grandfather William Pollexfen, with the great God himself.

What is it in his ancestors that stirs and shames the poet, as nearing fifty he draws up for "the story's end"? It is the vivid habits and powers he means by "the wasteful virtues." Roughly, he is claiming for his paternal line the wasteful virtues of learning, charity, bravery, patriotism; for his maternal line he claims enterprise and daring, habitual passionate vitality. It is a pattern loosely aristocratic, at least one form of nobility. The mercantile blood is not denied but it is sublimated; it "has not passed through any huckster's loin." In his view of them Yeats's mercantile ancestors were not shopkeepers; they would not (in Moll Flanders' idiom) have shown the mark of their hats upon their wigs, or the mark of their apron-strings upon their coats. They were shipmen and sailors, merchant-adventurers. William Pollexfen bears the scar of a whaling hook in his hand, hunts down enemies with a horsewhip, and displays in his little back parlor a painted coat of arms. When George Pollexfen rides to the race meeting at Sligo he is accompanied by two postilions in green livery.

The pattern is as well significantly Anglo-Irish, a strain after many generations in the land still not native or assimilated, still a bit alien and *rentier*. To be Anglo-Irish was to inherit a tradition of power and privilege, of landed gentility, of comparative wealth and culture, of Protestantism, of suspicious identification with the most hated of absentee proprietors, England herself. It was also to inherit the glory, though not necessarily the genius, of the most astonishingly brilliant and fertile strain in the history of British letters, the Anglo-Irish line that produced Congreve, Swift, Berkeley, Burke, Goldsmith, Sterne, Shaw, Wilde, Synge, Lady Gregory, Joyce Cary, and all the Yeatses.

The *grand seigneur* side of Yeats lasted all his life and if anything it intensified with time. It is the hardest side of him to like, at least for an American taste, which finds something repugnant and stagey in his tendency to love a lord, to admire power and privilege, and to adopt its magisterial manners. The elegance of his own genetic line was running thin by the time it reached his father's generation, and Yeats was perfectly capable of seeing as comedy the eccentricity of the older ones about him—of one grandfather who slept with a hatchet against burglars, of another who walked about jingling his keys so as not to surprise his servants in embarrassing attitudes, of the vain Protestant curate who ripped three pairs of skintight trousers before he could mount one horse: " 'I had hoped for a curate,' " his rector said, " 'but they have sent me a jockey.' "

Certainly John Butler Yeats's family could have had no illusions of wealth or stability. Their life was shabby and peripatetic, though never dull. J. B. Yeats was an admirable father and a gay and noble companion but a bad provider, and for many years everything anybody earned went perforce into what was called the family " 'swalley hole.' " Yeats speaks laconically of the "torn tackle" of his equipment, of inking his socks to hide the holes. For years, apparently, he was actually undernourished; by housing and feeding him in summers at Coole, Lady Gregory almost certainly extended his life. In view of these surrounding facts of his life, it is tempting to see Yeats's aristocratic leanings as wish-fulfilling and compensatory. One may be reminded of his own view of Keats in "Ego

Dominus Tuus" where *Ille*, who speaks for Yeats, says:

> His art is happy, but who knows his mind?
> I see a schoolboy when I think of him,
> With face and nose pressed to a sweet-shop window,
> For certainly he sank into his grave
> His senses and his heart unsatisfied,
> And made—being poor, ailing and ignorant,
> Shut out from all the luxury of the world,
> The coarse-bred son of a livery-stable keeper—
> Luxuriant song.

But Yeats's aristocracy, in this limited and conventional sense, was real and a thing of blood. As a young man he was poor and ailing and even ignorant; but he could never have been called coarse-bred. Yet all this is only a small and distracting part of what I mean by the nobility of Yeats, or of his own definition of nobility. The true nobility visible in the "Introductory Rhymes" is less a matter of wealth or breeding than a matter of spirit, a matter of feeling, a matter of noble passion. The wasteful virtues are deeds and feelings of passion and commitment, hot, unthinking and unselfish, generous. They have to do with blood only in the degree to which old blood is likely to be hot blood. The silent and fierce old man whom as a boy Yeats confused with God, as a man he identified with King Lear and thus with the order of wasteful virtues that informs high tragedy. "Even today," he writes in *Reveries*, "when I read *King Lear* his image is always before me and I often wonder if the delight in passionate men in my plays and in my poetry is more than his memory." Looking through the family miniatures collected by his sister Lily, who was the squirrel of the Yeats family, he reflected, ". . .I am delighted with all that joins my life to those who had power in Ireland or with those anywhere that were good servants and poor bargainers. . . ." To practice the wasteful virtues the thing most necessary is to possess

passion and generosity, to be a good servant and a poor
bargainer.

It is clear too that the emotion that ultimately drives this
poem, the poet's hopeless and unreconciled love for Maud
Gonne, though it is bitterly described as "a barren passion," is
of the order of nobility. Yeats's wasteful passion, good service
and a poor bargain, summons all the ramified nobility of the
poem. Maud was his Phoenix, his Helen, his daughter of the
swan, his Pallas Athene, his.woman Homer sung. To be so is to
be noble, and to feel so of a noble person is to join the line of
nobility. Such wasteful virtues earn the sun by kinship to it,
being luminous and fiery, sprung from what Yeats would later
call the resinous heart.

By the time of "The Tower," Yeats's roll-calling poem of
1926, his life was much altered, grander and more stable, in an
Ireland detached from England and dismembered in herself,
trying to become a modern state though barely alive after a
world war, a revolution, and a civil war. Ten years before he had
been confident and secure enough to refuse a knighthood,
quietly: "...I do not wish anyone to say of me, 'only for a
ribbon he left us.'" Yeats in 1926 was a senator of the Irish
Free State, an internationally famous man of letters, a Nobel
prizewinner who had been told that the Swedish royal family
preferred him to any other recipient of the prize because he had
the manners of a courtier. His inward elegance had moved
outward and confirmed itself in that graceful and imposing
presence that marked his deportment until the end of his life.
And for the first time he knew something like affluence.

His sisters, influenced by the ideals of archaism and
craftsmanship of William Morris, as was the poet who called
Morris "my chief of men," had prospered modestly in their
Cuala Industries, composed of Lily's fine needlework and

embroidery and Lolly's fine printing and illumination. Yeats spoke of the traditionary feeling that had quickly attached itself to the little Cuala volumes: "My sister's books are like an old family magazine. A few hundred people buy them all and expect a common theme. Only once did I put a book into the series that was not Irish—Ezra's Noh plays—and I had to write a long introduction to annex Japan to Ireland." Jack Yeats was becoming Ireland's best known modern painter, his work given mass and energy by his sympathy with the open-air life of Ireland, with fist-fighters and horsemen and seamen and the rambling tinkers of the roads. The poet kept finding in his brother's pictures faces he remembered from their boyhood on the Sligo quays fifty years before.

Old John Butler Yeats had come to be known in the family as their Pilgrim Father. He went to New York for a visit in 1908, liked it, and stayed on to try out a new incarnation. He had been called the best talker in Dublin, and he was soon known as the best talker in New York, where the competition was less severe. He kept ramshackle *salon* for a circle of writers and painters at his French boarding house on West 29th Street. John Sloan painted him there in "Yeats at Petitpas'," sketching and talking away to a little crowd about a dinner table in the back garden, in an attitude that recalls his son's image of him in a late poem, "his beautiful mischievous head thrown back." Ezra Pound recalled seeing "the father of all the Yeatsssssss" about 1910 riding an elephant at Coney Island. The new career of the old portrait painter was little more successful than the old. He wrote and lectured and painted, energetically and happily, but he never quite paid his way. He still suffered from his old incapacity to finish crucial pictures. He worked on a self-portrait at John Quinn's commission for ten years, and left it unfinished when he died, the paint by then a half-inch thick. His many letters to his children were vivid and homely documents, intensely human and intelligent; those to the poet particularly composing a piecemeal aesthetics and philosophy warm, original, and profound. W. B. Yeats was quite aware of his deep debt to his father's mind. Composing a lecture in 1910 he found himself working toward a thought which he recognized as his father's, and he reflected how often that had happened. "It made me realize with some surprise," he wrote, "how fully my philosophy of life has been inherited from you in all but its details and applications." Importuned many times to come home to Ireland, J. B. Yeats temporized and delayed, and finally died in New York in 1922 at the age of eighty-two. The son wrote soon after to Olivia Shakespear, "I find it hard to realize my father's death, he has so long been a mind to me, that mind seems to me still thinking and writing."

Meanwhile, still unwilling to substitute the book for the child, Yeats was seeking a wife and a home, a setting for a wife and child. Maud Gonne still refused him, and he turned to her beautiful young daughter Iseult, who also refused. Yeats then turned to Georgiana Hyde-Lees, a young woman half his age whom he had known for several years. She accepted and married him in 1917, and thenceforward she was his beloved George. It was a happy and fruitful marriage. "My wife is a perfect wife," Yeats wrote to Lady Gregory in December of 1917, "kind, wise, and unselfish. I think you were such another young girl once. She has made my life serene and full of order." In a few years George brought him a daughter, Anne, and a son, Michael. She brought him also, through her mediumship, through the "unknown instructors," those "reed-throated whisperers," the means to that ordering of his thought which became *A Vision*.

The physical house of Yeats had changed over these years

in what now seems a pattern, and one purposeful and
appropriate. His last close link with Sligo had been cut with the
death in 1910 of his beloved uncle George Pollexfen,
businessman, horseman, and astrologer. Lily, who had been in
attendance, reported that the banshee had cried on the night
before he died, and Yeats was comforted. Yeats had left the
family home in Bedford Park in London for the apartment in
Woburn Buildings which connected by a passage with the rooms
of Arthur Symons. At several intervals he shared a cottage in
Sussex with the brash young American Ezra Pound, who taught
him to fence, and to admire "certain noble plays of Japan," the
Noh plays, as expressions of an exotic aristocracy, models of
brevity and astringency and symbolism, of blood-nobility, an art
so simply noble that by it Yeats thought he might at last escape
all the paraphernalia of the commercial theatre, the claims of
audience. He wrote to John Quinn, "I had thought to escape
the press, and people digesting their dinners, and to write for
my friends." Such plays he considered might be played in a
drawing room or a barn. Those alternatives, the equality of the
drawing room and the barn, suggest what nobility was coming to
mean for Yeats. After his marriage there were long intervals at
Oxford, where Yeats worked in the Bodleian Library, finding it
the finest of all houses for the mind, "the most comfortable and
friendly library in the world and I suppose the most beautiful."
But George was equally horrified, he reported, by the hats and
the minds of the dons' wives. Summer after summer, before the
marriage, there had been Lady Gregory's modest great house at
Coole Park, in some ways the truest of all Yeats's spiritual
homes. For him it was the synthesis of the best of
Anglo-Ireland, where the widowed great Lady who had made
herself in middle age an artist and folklorist, heiress of a long
line of blood and wealth and power, herself at once lonely,

grand, and simple, attuned to any company in castle and cottage, presided over assorted spartan feasts of the spirit. His debt to her was incalculable, as he knew, and as he frequently and handsomely acknowledged.

Now, after 1916, there was the tower itself, literal and figurative, which gave the title to this poem and this volume. As always in Yeats's life, fact moved toward myth and symbol, and the tower invests his imagery for his last twenty years in a variety of attitudes, solemn or gay or mocking. Yeats acquired the tower for £ 35. The property consisted of an acre or so of land in the rolling countryside a few miles from Gort, from Coole Park, and from the sea, with a Norman stone tower and attached cottages, the whole half-ruinous. It is important to form an image of the parts and the whole, for all came together to form the emblem. The place is isolated in the countryside, set in the ell formed by a shallow little river flowing past one side and a narrow country road flowing over a stone bridge on another side. Thus it is of the land, of the water, of the road, and in its isolated verticality, of the sky. It is deep in Ireland and deep in time, the main structure dating back to feudal times. The immensely thick grey stone walls, pierced by slit windows, rise to form four stories and a battlement. Each story is a single huge square room, and the narrow winding stair of rough worn stone rises past each story to the roof. Yeats called the tower Thoor Ballylee, and he explained his logic in a letter to Olivia Shakespear: "Thoor is Irish for tower and it will keep people from suspecting us of modern gothic and a deer park. I think the harsh sound of 'Thoor' amends the softness of the rest."

Like the equation of drawing room and barn, that union of harsh and soft is what I want to get at, for it helps to explain the fluent functions of the symbol for Yeats. "My idea is to keep the contrast between the medieval castle and the peasant's cottage," he wrote. His nobility required both forms of life. "We shall live on the road like a country man, our white walled cottage with its border of flowers like any country cottage and then the gaunt castle," he said in a letter to Clement Shorter. To John Quinn he wrote of the tower in a vein of gay self-satire, "I am making a setting for my old age, a place to influence lawless youth, with its severity and antiquity." It occurred to him that had he possessed his tower earlier he might have been able to smooth Joyce's lawless and difficult way.

Yeats took the keenest pleasure in assuring the primitive integrity of the reconstruction and furnishing of the castle and the cottage. Local artisans—carpenters, masons, smiths—were to do all the work, overseen by a local builder named Raftery, an emotional man who wept when things went wrong. Massive handmade tables, chairs, and beds were designed by Scott, whom Yeats usually referred to as a "drunken man of genius." Because building materials could not be had in war time, Yeats triumphantly bought the wreckage of an old mill, "great beams and three-inch planks, and old paving stones." And finally he composed one of his brutal short lyrics, "To Be Carved on a Stone at Thoor Ballylee," as his own part in the country artisanship.

> I, the poet William Yeats,
> With old mill boards and sea-green slates,
> And smithy work from the Gort forge,
> Restored this tower for my wife George;
> And may these characters remain
> When all is ruin once again.

He had bought the house, as he put it in "Meditations in Time of Civil War," "for an old neighbour's friendship," "and decked and altered it for a girl's love." For this, in its gracefully

ponderous way, was also a honeymoon cottage: "Beauty and
fool together laid," as he was to put it later. And that
conjunction, too, suggests the poles of Yeats's nobility.

It is the conjunction I wish to speak of in the poem, the
seemingly disjunct series of images and ideas that come in train
to the poet's mind as he paces upon the battlements of the
tower to "send imagination forth/ Under the day's declining
beam, and call/ Images and memories/ From ruin or from
ancient trees. . . ." First he recalls an elegant Mrs. French,
cruelly lofty:

> Beyond that ridge lived Mrs. French, and once
> When every silver candlestick or sconce
> Lit up the dark mahogany and the wine,
> A serving-man, that could divine
> That most respected lady's every wish,
> Ran and with the garden shears
> Clipped an insolent farmer's ears
> And brought them in a little covered dish.

Immediately, without hesitation, the mind moves to a nameless
peasant girl, celebrated for her beauty by a blind folk poet, and
the men maddened by poetry and wine and love who set out to
find her by moonlight: "And one was drowned in the great bog
of Cloone." He pauses to reflect on the phenomenon of a blind
poet admiring a girl's beauty, but leaps at once to the oneness
and inextricableness of human passion:

> Strange, but the man who made the song was blind;
> Yet, now I have considered it, I find
> That nothing strange; the tragedy began
> With Homer that was a blind man,
> And Helen has all living hearts betrayed.

And he recalls that he himself had behaved as oddly as the blind
poet Raftery, in creating Hanrahan and sending him off to
follow a hare and hounds made from a pack of cards, so that

"he stumbled, tumbled, fumbled to and fro/ And had but broken knees for hire/ And horrible splendour of desire." The mind now swings home to the tower itself, the history or legend of its occupants: "an ancient bankrupt," harried to death, rough men-at-arms who "climbed the narrow stair" "cross-gartered to the knees/ Or shod in iron," or certain ghostly men-at-arms who interrupted sleepers with the noise of their great wooden dice.

It is a fantastic roll that Yeats is calling. Those who are summoned form a company in being ancient, local, and passionate, a nobility of fire and commitment, the kind of folk who might be hoped to have an answer to a certain disastrous question about to be asked by the present master of the house:

> As I would question all, come all who can;
> Come old, necessitous, half-mounted man;
> And bring beauty's blind rambling celebrant;
> The red man the juggler sent
> Through God-forsaken meadows; Mrs. French,
> Gifted with so fine an ear;
> The man drowned in a bog's mire,
> When mocking Muses chose the country wench.

What Yeats at past sixty-one wants to know is whether all of them were tortured as he is by the passing of time and the losing of life:

> Did all old men and women, rich and poor,
> Who trod upon these rocks or passed this door,
> Whether in public or in secret rage
> As I do now against old age?

But a noble old man of property ought to make a will, and that is what Yeats does in the long trimeter paragraphs that close out the poem. The property he bequeaths, however, is primarily spiritual, more ideal than real. Having prepared his peace with learning and poetry and love, "all those things

whereof/ Man makes a superhuman/ Mirror-resembling dream,"
what he has left to bequeath are his pride and his faith. His
pride is Irish but super-political, brave, free, generous,
impassioned:

> The pride of people that were
> Bound neither to Cause nor to State,
> Neither to slaves that were spat on,
> Nor to the tyrants that spat,
> The people of Burke and of Grattan
> That gave, though free to refuse—
> Pride, like that of the morn,
> When the headlong light is loose,
> Or that of the fabulous horn,
> Or that of the sudden shower
> When all streams are dry,
> Or that of the hour
> When the swan must fix his eye
> Upon a fading gleam,
> Float out upon a long
> Last reach of glimmering stream
> And there sing his last song.

His faith is religious but unchristian, an assertion of the power
of man's impassioned will to force upon life and death a
sufficient shape and significance:

> I mock Plotinus' thought
> And cry in Plato's teeth,
> Death and life were not
> Till man made up the whole,
> Made lock, stock and barrel
> Out of his bitter soul,
> Aye, sun and moon and star, all.
> And further add to that
> That, being dead, we rise,
> Dream and so create
> Translunar Paradise.

And who are Yeats's heirs? Ordinary noble men, young, active, self-defined, lonely integrities:

> . . .upstanding men
> That climb the streams until
> The fountain leap, and at dawn
> Drop their cast at the side
> Of dripping stone. . . .

Like the tower itself, the poem is a ramshackle monolith, casually impregnable, held together, really, by the noble old energy of complex but purified passion.

"The Municipal Gallery Revisited" of Yeats's *Last Poems* is a roll-calling poem of a more specific and consistent kind. The poet must be seen as an old man communing alone with racial shades, "the images of thirty years," the ancestors of modern Ireland. It is the portraits that seize and hold him, significant countenances, dead but speaking. There are the patriots, political men, Casement, Griffith, O'Higgins. There is the face of a nameless woman, "beautiful and gentle in her Venetian way," whom he remembers seeing "all but fifty years ago/ For twenty minutes in some studio." Thinking of time and passion and beauty and sacrifice, the old poet is invaded by a sudden unbidden wave of feeling, shaken to the point of tears: "Heart-smitten with emotion I sink down,/ My heart recovering with covered eyes." Touching in its privacy and impressive in its susceptibility, that vision surprises Yeats's noble nature in action for us, defined by the capacity to feel and to value noble bearing and noble work to the base of his being.

Yeats's eyes move next to images of the Coole Park line, Lady Gregory, her son Robert Gregory, her nephew Hugh Lane. All are dead in fact but live on in feeling in a way the canvas cannot contain: "But where is the brush that could show anything/ Of all that pride and that humility?" Yeats asks. Pride and humility: once again it is the fusion at the center of the nobility he loved, hymned, and embodied. All the Gregorys are gone and even the great house is gone where, as he puts it, "honour had lived so long." But this mechanical passing he cannot mourn. The life of that house had a quality that lives on superior to the envy of time and of fresher, smaller motives. "No fox can foul the lair the badger swept."

That was, Yeats parenthesizes, "an image out of Spenser and the common tongue." Once more it is the noble conjunction of the elegant, the ancient, the traditional, the common. Now Yeats collects the images of the trinity he wished might have stood together to receive the Nobel Prize, himself, John Synge, Lady Gregory, now forever united in his feeling in the common-noble "dream of the noble and the beggar-man."

> John Synge, I and Augusta Gregory, thought
> All that we did, all that we said or sang
> Must come from contact with the soil, from that
> Contact everything Antaeus-like grew strong.
> We three alone in modern times had brought
> Everything down to that sole test again,
> Dream of the noble and the beggar-man.

Yeats moves finally to Synge's own image, whom he describes only in the packed phrase, "that rooted man." "Think where man's glory most begins and ends," he invites us at the end of the poem, "and say my glory was I had such friends." Man's glory most begins and ends in high passions, rising out of the common life and wishing finally to speak only to that. In the spring of 1937 Yeats commended an essay on his work by Archibald MacLeish as "the only article on the subject which has not bored me for years." MacLeish had praised the diction of his poetry as "public." "That word, which I had not thought of myself, is a word I want," Yeats wrote to Lady Dorothy Wellesley. Thinking earlier of his ideal auditor, his Connemara fisherman, Yeats had cried,

> . . .'Before I am old
> I shall have written him one
> Poem maybe as cold
> And passionate as the dawn.

That is why the tower had to rise out of the stream and the
earth, and why the cottages had to remain at its base, to tie it
Antaeus-like to the soil, to prevent its wish to soar off into the
lofty and the abstract.

Two final Irish houses of Yeats require brief mention. Each
in its way preserves the unity of the pattern of his habitation.
Early in 1922, with the tower still barely habitable only in
summer, George Yeats tired fatally of the hats of the dons'
wives in Oxford and resolved to find a house in Dublin. "My
Saturn suggested delay but her Mars carried it and she went,"
Yeats wrote to Olivia Shakespear. Again their luck held and Mrs.
Yeats found at a bargain a fine tall Georgian house at 82
Merrion Square. With some complacency Yeats explained to Mrs.
Shakespear that Merrion Square was to Dublin what Berkeley
Square was to London. The house had been built about 1740
with rooms "very large and stately" and handsome mantelpieces.
Yeats felt, he wrote, "very grand" remembering a street ballad
about the Duke of Wellington: " 'In Merrion Square/ This noble
hero first drew breath/ Amid a nation's cheers.' " It was an
elegant house, withal plain, an appropriate setting for a man
who within the next year was to be a senator of Ireland, a D. Litt.
of Trinity College, Dublin, and a holder of the Nobel Prize.

In May of 1932 Lady Gregory died. Yeats wrote, "I have
lost one who has been to me for nearly forty years my strength
and my conscience." At Coole he heard a ragged Dublin sculptor
who had called to pay his respects, musing, after staring about

him at the pictures of the great who had been associated with that house, " 'All the nobility of earth.' " "I felt he did not mean it for that room alone but for lost tradition," Yeats wrote. He continued: "How much of my own work has not been but the repetition of those words." In the same summer Yeats occupied his last Irish house, smaller and more simplified like life itself for him. What he called "this little creeper-covered farm-house" was named 'Riversdale' and was situated in Rathfarnham, "just too far from Dublin to go there without good reason and too far, I hope, for most interviewers and the less determined travelling bores." For Edith Shackleton Heald he drew a plan of his study and went on to describe it:

> All round the study walls are book-cases but some stop half way up and over them are pictures by my brother, my father, by Robert Gregory. On each side of the window into [the] flower garden are two great Chinese pictures (Dulac's gift) and in the window into the greenhouse hangs a most lovely Burne-Jones window (Ricketts's gift). Through the glass door into the flower garden I see the bare boughs of apple trees and a few last flowers. . . .

Through French doors he would walk out into the garden to "share the gooseberries with the bullfinches." Outside there was space for fruit trees, croquet and tennis lawns, and a bowling green.

This is an elegant simplicity, but a simplicity, and it was in a real sense a return to the earth, an Antaeus-gesture. Yeats thought of 'Riversdale' as a last place in life. "We have a lease for but thirteen years but that will see me out of life," he wrote to Mrs. Shakespear. Violent poetic work went on in this quiet place, the splendid extravagance of passion of the final lyrical flowing-out of the poet self-defined as "foolish, passionate man," "a wild old wicked man." We can watch the house itself erupt into grand romantic passion within a single poem, "An Acre of Grass."

Picture and book remain,
An acre of green grass
For air and exercise,
Now strength of body goes;
Midnight, an old house
Where nothing stirs but a mouse.

My temptation is quiet.
Here at life's end
Neither loose imagination,
Nor the mill of the mind
Consuming its rag and bone,
Can make the truth known.

Grant me an old man's frenzy,
Myself must I remake
Till I am Timon and Lear
Or that William Blake
Who beat upon the wall
Till Truth obeyed his call;

A mind Michael Angelo knew
That can pierce the clouds,
Or inspired by frenzy
Shake the dead in their shrouds;
Forgotten else by mankind,
An old man's eagle mind.

"Passion to me is the essential," Yeats had written. In a letter to
Wyndham Lewis he made clear what passion meant to him,
highly defined; he spoke of "passion ennobled by intensity, by
endurance, by wisdom. We had it in one man once. He lies in
St. Patrick's now under the greatest epitaph in history." The
reference of course is to Jonathan Swift.

One who had followed Yeats's own accumulation of
passion ennobled by intensity, by endurance, by wisdom, might
barely have hoped for something so magnificent at the end as
the "bitter and gay" *Last Poems*. It is now that he forms such

creatures as Crazy Jane and Tom the Lunatic and John Kinsella lamenting for his old bawd Mrs. Mary Moore. This is Old Man Yeats content at last to "lie down where all the ladders start,/ In the foul rag-and-bone shop of the heart." Looking about him at the anarchic modern landscape where once again there's a light in Troy, the world "turning and turning in the widening gyre," where "things fall apart; the center cannot hold," he reacts in a brilliant saturnine irony, a cackling approving curse, a kind of affirmative for which he finds his own proper phrase, "tragic joy."

> Irrational streams of blood are staining earth;
> Empedocles has thrown all things about;
> Hector is dead and there's a light in Troy;
> We that look on but laugh in tragic joy.

"What matter?" he inquires. "Out of cavern come a voice,/ And all it knows is that one word 'Rejoice!' "

"For laughter too is a passion," as Longinus affirmed long ago. Noble men, in any case, are not going to submit to the death of nobility.

> Those that Rocky Face holds dear,
> Lovers of horses and of women, shall
> From marble of a broken sepulchre,
> Or dark betwixt the polecat and the owl,
> Or any rich, dark nothing disinter
> The workman, noble and saint, and all things run
> On that unfashionable gyre again.

What he is involved in, the old poet sees, is simply life, the recurrent native forms of experience, a time of the time of man. It has all happened before and will happen again, with tears and laughter.

> On their own feet they came, or on shipboard,
> Camel-back, horse-back, ass-back, mule-back,

> Old civilisations put to the sword.
> Then they and their wisdom went to rack:
> No handiwork of Callimachus,
> Who handled marble as if it were bronze,
> Made draperies that seemed to rise
> When sea-wind swept the corner, stands;
> His long lamp-chimney shaped like the stem
> Of a slender palm, stood but a day;
> All things fall and are built again
> And those that build them again are gay.

Perhaps the strangest, truest, most exhilarating shape Yeats found to embody his last nobility is the stilt-walking hero of "High Talk." He is a lofty clown-figure, both artist and artisan, both man and myth, both father and child. He is an extravagant attenuation, teetering, grimacing, just dangerously controlled on the edge of unreason, a funny and terrible fusion of Yeats's central conjunctions: workman and noble and saint, hunchback and saint and fool. He is all metaphor, Malachi, stilts and all. Earlier Yeats had spoken of art as "but a vision of reality"; now, even in the prose of his letters, he is using such phrases as "the madness of vision." Here is the whole poem, which is among other things a travesty of a Petrarchan sonnet, in octave and sestet, but rhymed in couplets, and cast in long snaky hexameters of dactyl and anapest:

> Processions that lack high stilts have nothing that catches the eye.
> What if my great-granddad had a pair that were twenty foot high,
> And mine were but fifteen foot, no modern stalks upon higher,
> Some rogue of the world stole them to patch up a fence or a fire.
> Because piebald ponies, led bears, caged lions, make but poor shows,
> Because children demand Daddy-long-legs upon his timber toes,
> Because women in the upper storeys demand a face at the pane,
> That patching old heels they may shriek, I take to chisel and plane.
>
> Malachi Stilt-Jack am I, whatever I learned has run wild,
> From collar to collar, from stilt to stilt, from father to child.

All metaphor, Malachi, stilts and all. A barnacle goose
Far up in the stretches of night; night splits and the dawn
   breaks loose;
I, through the terrible novelty of light, stalk on, stalk on;
Those great sea-horses bare their teeth and laugh at the dawn.

The speaker of those lines has news for the Delphic Oracle. His is a vision that sees so much, so far, so wide, so high, and so deep that it must be mad. It rises out of the vision of life as tragedy but expresses itself as satyr-comedy. Those eyes, those ancient glittering eyes, are gay. I suggest that the poem lays out, with splendid angularity, the limits and the main members of the nobility of the house of Yeats. It is traditional and familial, it has run wild from father to child, it inherits (almost) the heroic height of a twenty-foot great-granddad. It makes its own vestment by its own craft applying its own tools to its own cheap native materials: it takes to chisel and plane. It stretches the human figure presumptuously, grandly, and comically toward the sky without ever losing touch of the earth: Daddy-long-legs upon his timber toes. It is sophisticated and innocent. Its function is to make shows, processions, to leer upon children and men and women at their ordinary work with astonishing grimaces from surprising heights. And then to stalk on through the terrible novelty of light to the place where night splits and the dawn breaks loose.

In the postscript of a letter to Ethel Mannin a few months before he died, Yeats wrote of the arrangements he was making for his burial. "It will be in a little remote country churchyard in Sligo, where my great grandfather was the clergyman a hundred years ago." He quoted the now famous lines from "Under Ben Bulben" which he designed for his epitaph: " 'Cast a cold eye/ On life, on death;/ Horseman, pass by.' " Typically, at the end, Yeats wished to lie down where all his ladders started. When he spoke of his plans to his sister Lily she commented drily, " 'This is a break with tradition. There has not been a tombstone in the Yeats family since the eighteenth century. The family has always been very gay.' " The Yeats habit, he explained to Edith Shackleton Heald, was to "let the grass grow over the dead and speak of them no more." The tombstone would be a ceremonious addition, but in Sligo churchyard Yeats would still be robed in the long friends.

Among those stilt-walkers who are poets, no modern stalks upon higher ground than Yeats. And not many ancients. What he shares with the other greatest poets is uniqueness. In the long run he is only himself, self-defined—self-born, after all. He mocks our enterprise, though we must do our best to praise him.